BEYOND PLACEMENT
Mothers View Foster Care

Shirley Jenkins and Elaine Norman

Based on the most extensive research into foster care ever undertaken, this book presents an important new picture of families whose children have been placed in foster care.

In an earlier companion study, *Filial Deprivation and Foster Care,* Shirley Jenkins and Elaine Norman reported on the results of interviews of parents of more than 600 foster children 90 days after their placement and formulated the innovative concept of filial deprivation to complement that of maternal deprivation. In this impressive follow-up study, the authors present the long-term information gleaned from a five-year longitudinal investigation of mothers of children placed in foster homes. The work is distinguished for making available significant new material of relevance to many areas of social service.

One of its major contributions is the emphasis put on reasons for placement, focusing on what are defined as socially approved and socially unacceptable reasons. The authors' findings in this area lead them to call for the development of a "no-fault" foster care system available to all as needed, and strong evidence is provided in support of this proposal. This study is also noteworthy for incorporating clients' evaluation of services and for reporting changes in maternal feelings about placement at the time of entry as compared with the time of discharge. Two areas explored for the first time in this study are the role expectations of mothers

in relation to caseworkers and the mothers' perceptions of what a family means and how family constellations relate to household composition.

Growing out of the well-known Family Welfare Research Program of the Columbia University School of Social Work, *Beyond Placement* is the most systematic book yet written on parents whose children are in placement. The authors' delineation of the practice implications of their findings makes this work especially valuable for foster care agencies and personnel and other practitioners. Child welfare researchers will depend upon the book as a basic study.

Social Work
Social Issues Series
Columbia University
School of Social Work

Shirley Jenkins is a professor in the Columbia University School of Social Work and chairman of the doctoral program there. She has written many articles and several books on child welfare. **Elaine Norman** is associate professor at the Graduate School of Social Service of Fordham University.

Beyond Placement

Mothers View Foster Care

Shirley Jenkins
and Elaine Norman

1975

Columbia University Press · New York and London

Shirley Jenkins is a professor and chairman of the doctoral program at the Columbia University School of Social Work. Elaine Norman is an associate professor at the Graduate School of Social Service, Fordham University.

Library of Congress Cataloging in Publication Data

Jenkins, Shirley.
  Beyond placement.

  Includes index.
  1. Foster home care—New York (City) 2. Family—
New York (City)—Longitudinal studies. I. Norman,
Elaine, joint author. II. Title.
HV875.J44   362.7'33'097471   75-15916
ISBN 0-231-03812-7

The Columbia University School of Social Work publication series, "Social Work and Social Issues," is concerned with the implications of social work practice and social welfare policy for solving problems. Each volume is an independent work. The series is intended to contribute to the knowledge base of social work education, to facilitate communication with related disciplines, and to serve as a background for public policy discussion. Other books in the series are

Shirley Jenkins, *editor*
Social Security in International Perspective 1969

George Brager and Harry Specht
Community Organizing 1973

Alfred J. Kahn, *editor*
Shaping the New Social Work 1973

Foreword

Beyond Placement: Mothers View Foster Care by Drs. Shirley Jenkins and Elaine Norman is the thoughtful second volume of findings from the Family Welfare Research Program. As such, it is part of an extensive program of foster-care studies carried out over the last decade at Columbia University School of Social Work.

This volume, like the earlier one, *Filial Deprivation and Foster Care,* stems from a five-year longitudinal study of families whose children entered foster care in 1966 in New York City. One of the real values of these two books is their focus on the family and the attitudes of the parents involved. Also, at a time when considerable emphasis is being placed on evaluation of services, the authors devoted appropriate emphasis to the responses and reactions of the consumers. How mothers judge foster care and social services is clearly not the total answer to problems of evaluation, but consumer attitudes and responses toward these and other services deserve much more attention than they have received up to now.

At the end of the five-year period, about 75 percent of the children placed in foster care had been discharged, primarily to their own homes. Generally speaking, the attitudes of mothers toward placement were somewhat more positive than they had been earlier, but by and large the economic and social conditions of the families had shown little if any improvement. One interesting sidelight discussed by the authors is that 10 mothers had moved off AFDC as a result of employment; however, in 9 of these situations the child involved was still in foster care. While the numbers are too small to derive any significant conclusions, they may well point to another of these all too frequent conflicts and contradictions between and among our programs.

One of the major contributions made by this book is the emphasis placed on reasons for placement, with the focus on what are defined as socially approved and socially unacceptable reasons. Which category a family fits into makes a considerable difference in how a mother feels about placement and about the service and workers involved. Even more important is that it also seems to affect the way the worker reacts to the client and the kinds of services families and children receive. The inequity and injustice of such an approach are self-evident but unfortunately all too real. Dr. Jenkins and Dr. Norman call for the development of a "no-fault" foster care system available to all as needed. The authors make a strong case for their proposal and offer appropriate supporting evidence. Now it becomes the task of all of us to work to translate this effective study into meaningful national social policy.

MITCHELL I. GINSBERG
Dean, Columbia University School of Social Work

Acknowledgments

The acknowledgments for this longitudinal study, which has spanned ten years of planning, research, and writing, express appreciation to those who have made long-term commitments to our research enterprise. In this second volume reporting findings, we continue to be grateful to those agencies and persons named in our first volume, *Filial Deprivation and Foster Care*. Support was received initially from the Children's Bureau, and later from the Community Services Administration, Social and Rehabilitation Service, both of the U.S. Department of Health, Education, and Welfare. In particular we express our gratitude to Dr. Charles P. Gershenson and Dr. Abraham S. Levine, who facilitated the conduct of our official business.

Throughout its duration this study was housed at the Columbia University School of Social Work, and had the unfailing support of Mitchell I. Ginsberg, Dean; Sidney Berengarten, Associate Dean; and Samuel Finestone, Director of the Center for Research and Demonstration. Among our colleagues on the companion Child Welfare Research Program, we have had close collaborative relationships with Dr. David Fanshel, Dr. Eugene B. Shinn and Dr. Deborah Shapiro. We continue to depend on the wise consultation of Dr. Leonard S. Kogan. In our work important contributions were made by two staff research associates, Mallory Pepper and Rosalind Zitner, both of whom supervised the field interviews and worked on data processing and analysis. In addition, Mallory Pepper prepared the index for this volume. We are grateful for the technical assistance of Mary Elizabeth Smith and Dianne Carton, who helped prepare both volumes for the press.

Basic data for the study were obtained with the collaboration of the Bureau of Child Welfare, New York City Department of Social Services, and the Family Court of the State of New York. The field work was done by a sensitive and dedicated staff of social work interviewers. We all express our gratitude to the families of the children in foster care who gave so generously of their time and experiences.

SHIRLEY JENKINS AND ELAINE NORMAN

New York
May 1975

Contents

Beyond Placement

Mothers View Foster Care

One

Study Concepts and Design

The placement of children in foster homes and institutions is a partial, rather than a comprehensive, social service. Although care and sometimes treatment are provided for neglected, dependent, and disturbed children, the help given to meet total family needs is problematic, varying with agency policy and capability and with the nature of the difficulties.

What happens to families while children are in care, and after they are discharged? When the crisis has passed, what are the chronic needs that persist? The research findings reported here are based on a longitudinal study of families of placed children, and show changes that occurred in the circumstances of these families over the five years after initial foster care. Changes in maternal feelings about placement are also reported and compared with mothers' feelings on entry, as well as with their feelings when children are discharged.

How do mothers evaluate foster care, and what uses have they made of social services in coping with family problems? This study joins the small but growing social work literature that incorporates clients' evaluations of services, and clients' responses to presumed "help," as a significant part of its research findings. These evaluations go beyond foster care and include the total range of available social services.

In addition to change data and client evaluations, two new areas are reported. The first deals with role expectations of mothers in relation to caseworkers, or how mothers think social workers expect them to behave in the casework interview. The second explores concepts and definitions of family. New data are reported on mothers' perceptions of what a family means, and of how family constellations relate to household composition.

The present report is the second volume of findings arising from the Family Welfare Research Program. This study is a longitudinal investigation of families in New York City whose children entered foster care in 1966. Baseline data on their situations at the time of placement have been reported in the first book published from this research, *Filial Deprivation and Foster Care*.[1] That book contains information on living conditions, poverty status, and family background of the study sample, and substantial attention was paid to reasons children entered care. Social attitudes and parental feelings were discussed at length. Several key concepts were introduced, which will be briefly noted later in this chapter. These included the categories for classifying reasons for placement, the scale of socioeconomic circumstances, the concept of filial deprivation, and the formulation of social attitudes and attitudes toward agencies.

This second volume is not an updating of the first, although change data are included, but it represents a new approach to a substantially expanded information base. The first book reported data from the initial interview in 1966, the year children in the study sample entered care. The new data in the present book are the results of two follow-up interviews held in 1968 and 1971 with mothers of

[1] Shirley Jenkins and Elaine Norman, *Filial Deprivation and Foster Care* (New York: Columbia University Press, 1972).

placed children, in which there was some repetition of earlier questions but also the introduction of new areas of inquiry.

The research is part of an extensive program of foster care studies undertaken at the Columbia University School of Social Work over the 10 years from 1964 to 1974.[2] The initial study sample was composed of 624 children from 467 families, from birth to age 12 years, who experienced their first placement in New York City between January and October 1966. Children came into the study as they entered care, but did not become part of the sample until they had been in care for 90 days.[3]

Three major studies were undertaken on the overall sample. The family research, reported here, studied the biological families of the children. The child welfare research undertook a comprehensive study of the children, including repeated psychological testing, school reports, and behavioral ratings. The agency research conducted intensive investigation of agency input and outcome.[4] The entire program benefited from substantial cooperation by the Bureau of Child Welfare of the New York City Department of Social Services (formerly the Department of Welfare), the Family Court, and over 80 child-caring agencies in New York City.

FAMILY INTERVIEW CONTENT

Information for the family study was gathered in three field interviews in 1966, 1968, and 1971. In the initial interview mothers, fathers, and other child-caring persons were interviewed in their homes by trained

[2] The program was supported by the U.S. Department of Health, Education and Welfare, initially by the Children's Bureau, Office of Child Development, and later by the Social and Rehabilitation Services.

[3] The sample was limited to children who entered the foster care system. The following categories were excluded: children designated by the courts as juvenile delinquents or PINS (Persons in Need of Supervision), children placed in institutions for the physically handicapped or the mentally retarded, and children admitted to psychiatric hospitals.

[4] The child welfare research data are being reported by Drs. David Fanshel and Eugene B. Shinn, in *Children in Foster Care,* and the agency data by Dr. Deborah Shapiro, in *Agencies and Children: A Child Welfare Network's Investment in its Clients,* two volumes to be published by Columbia University Press.

social workers. In follow-up interviews, where changes in circumstances and responses were stressed, emphasis was placed on interviews with mothers, since they were the most accessible and knowledgeable respondents and the key child-caring adults.

In the three study interviews, there were several categories of questions. Basic demographic material (such as ethnic group, birthdate, and birthplace), once secured, was not requested again. Information on areas such as income, housing, attitudes to agencies, and feelings on placement was requested in all three interviews, so that change data could be obtained. The investigations into the new areas of inquiry, maternal role expectations and family concepts, were made in the second and third field interviews, respectively. Chart 1 indicates the discrete and continuing areas of content investigated in each of the three field interviews.

Study Sample over Time

The study sample varied over time, and as expected was reduced by attrition over the five years from 390 to 257 families interviewed. The initial figures for the overall study were 624 children from 467 families, some families having two children in placement.[5] Not all these families were included in the family study sample, however, since by the time the field interviewing began, three months after placement, 26 of the mothers had decided to surrender children for adoption and it was considered inappropriate to visit these cases. In 11 additional cases mothers were not approached because of agency requests to postpone interviews for casework reasons. Of the 430 families appropriate for the field survey, 390 cases, or 91 percent, were interviewed in their homes in the initial survey, and there were only 21 refusals and 19 cases who could not be located.

---

[5] If more than two children from any one family entered care, only two, selected at random, became part of the sample.

Chart 1. Areas Covered in Family Welfare Research Program Interviews

CONTENT AREA	FIRST INTERVIEW (6 months after entry)	SECOND INTERVIEW (2 1/2 years after entry)	THIRD INTERVIEW (5 years after entry)

PLACEMENT EXPERIENCE	1. Precipitating problems
	2. Paternal feelings
	  a) On day of placement
	  b) On having child in placement
		1. State of placement problems
		2.....................................►
		
		  b).............................►
		
		  c) On day of discharge
		  d) On having had child in placement
			1...............................►
			2...............................►
			
			  b)............................►
			
			  c)............................►
			  d)............................►

AGENCY RELATED ATTITUDES AND EXPERIENCES	1. Attitude toward agencies
	  a) Facilitator
	  b) Usurper
	  c) Surrogate
	2. Necessity of placement
	3. Effect on child, self
	4. Contacts with child during placement
		1...............................►
		  a).............................►
		  b).............................►
		  c).............................►
		2...............................►
		3...............................►
		4...............................►
		
		5. Contacts with workers
		6. Help, problems, from workers
		7. Parent involvement in discharge planning
		8. Mother's role expectations
			1...............................►
			  a).............................►
			  b).............................►
			  c).............................►
			2...............................►
			3...............................►
			4...............................►
			
			5...............................►
			6...............................►
			
			7...............................►
			
			9. Parental perception of child's feelings about placement
			10. Worker contacts after discharge

GENERAL ATTITUDES	1. Related to children
	  a) Expectations for child
	  b) Preferred child traits
	  c) Child-rearing practice
	2. Conception of parenthood
	3. Marital role expectations
	4. Marital role performances
	5. Social attitudes
	  a) Alienation
	  b) Trust
	  c) Calculation
		2...............................►
		
		5...............................►
		  a).............................►
			2...............................►
			
			5...............................►
			  a).............................►

FAMILY FUNCTIONING AND DEFINITIONS		1. Child's behavior problems 2. Child's contacts with natural father 3. Contact between natural parents 4. Parent acceptance of child 5. Household solidarity 6. Relationships outside household	1...............................► 2...............................► 3...............................► 7. Definition of "family" 8. People "family" includes
COMMUNITY RESOURCES AND PRIMARY PREVENTION		1. Nature of service received 2. Contact initiator	1...............................► 2...............................► 3. Community services received 4. Community group contacts 5. Parental proposals for preventive services
SOCIOECONOMIC AND DEMOGRAPHIC INFORMATION	1. Source, amount income 2. Education 3. Housing 4. Household composition 5. Marital status 6. Religion 7. Ethnic group 8. Age 9. Place of birth	1...............................► 2...............................► 3...............................► 4...............................► 5...............................►	1...............................► 2...............................► 3...............................► 4...............................► 5...............................► 10. Employment history

► Indicates continuing investigation of content area

At the time of the second interview, two and one-half years later, there were 389 families considered to be appropriate for field survey, of whom 304 families were interviewed. At that time there were 28 refusals and 57 cases that could not be located. By 1971, five years after placement, further attrition had occurred, with 324 cases remaining in the field operation. Of these, 257 were interviewed, and there were 17 refusals and 50 families who could not be located. The full report on the sample over time is shown in table 1, by cases and respondents.

Table 1. Field Operations for the Family Study

Cases	Time					
	I (1966)		II (1968)		III (1971)	
	Number	Percent	Number	Percent	Number	Percent
Included: Total	430	100	389	100	324	100
Interviewed [a]	390	91	304	78	257	79
Not interviewed	40	9	85	22	67	21
Refusal	21	5	28	7	17	5
Unable to locate	19	4	57	15	50	16
Excluded: Total	37	100	78	100	143	100
Adoption	26	70	32	41	44	31
Casework reasons (agency request)	11	30	21	27	23	16
Previous refusal	—	—	15	19	45	31
Previously unable to locate	—	—	8	10	27	19
Child deceased	—	—	2	3	4	3
Respondent: Total	390	100	304	100	257	100
Mother	297	76	243	80	186	72
Other [b]	93	24	61	20	71	28

[a] For 88 cases, both mother and father were interviewed separately. Some fathers were seen in the initial family interview, others in a special father survey that followed, bringing total of fathers seen to 137, including 88 interviews of both parents and 49 of fathers alone.

[b] Primarily fathers and other relatives.

Considering the social characteristics of the study sample, including poverty, substantial emotional instability, family dysfunction, physical illness of many mothers, and frequent moves of households, some loss of contact could be expected. In addition, the study period was one of substantial urban renewal activity, with interviewers reporting whole blocks where clients had lived at the time of previous interviews as being leveled to rubble. Thus the usual contacts of neighbors, superintendents, and local stores with information on where to reach respondents were just not available. This added to the problems of follow-up.

Two further issues in sample size relate to the purpose of the analysis and the designation of the respondent. At the time of placement only 11 percent of the children in the study sample of 390 families were living in intact homes with both parents. The largest number, 40 percent, were living with their mothers without fathers in the home. Other children lived with fathers, grandparents, other relatives, or friends. The initial study decision was to designate mothers as primary respondents to the study interview, but if mothers were not available, first fathers and then other relatives or child-caring persons were interviewed. In the initial interview survey, 297 mothers were seen, representing 76 percent of all respondents. Because of the importance of securing paternal responses to the placement situation, a special father interview was undertaken. Together with those seen earlier, a total of 137 biological fathers of placed children were interviewed, whether or not they were living with the child under study. A special analysis of the correspondence between responses of mothers and fathers, both living together and living apart, was made in the first study volume.[6]

The difficulties of reaching fathers, and the distance of many from the children's situation, led to the decision that in follow-up interviews the emphasis would be on securing responses from mothers. They were closest to the children, most knowledgeable about the fam-

---

[6] Jenkins and Norman, *Filial Deprivation,* chapter 6, "Parental Pairs," pp. 191–225.

ily circumstances, and clearly the most significant figures in the future lives of the children. The study was designed so that several of the question areas focused specifically on matters that could be answered only by mothers. Among these areas were maternal feelings, attitudes, role expectations, and evaluations of foster care services from direct experiences. The distribution of interviews by respondent is shown in chart 2. The study methodology in this respect reflects the prevailing pattern, which is that the large majority of children who enter foster care are being reared in single-parent, mother-headed households.

In the second full field operation, 243 mothers were interviewed, or 80 percent of all respondents. Finally, in the third interview, 186 mothers were seen, 72 percent of all respondents. The responses of these 186 mothers on evaluation of placement are reported in this volume. However, 26 of these mothers had not been interviewed at the time of the initial study, being ill, institutionalized, or not available. The analysis of change data is therefore limited to the 160 mothers interviewed initially and also five years later.

Although the mothers seen at the third interview represent a substantial drop in number from those seen initially,this is typical of longitudinal field studies, especially where severe pathology and extensive mobility are characteristic of the sample. As many as ten field visits were made in some cases to find elusive respondents. The social work field interviewers included Black, white, and Puerto Rican staff,[7] and approximately one-third of all interviews were conducted in Spanish.

[7] "Black" and "Puerto Rican" are used in this volume to refer to names of ethnic groups. Ethnicity is not a precise concept with clear boundaries, but it is nonetheless a viable one, implying a combination of some or all of the following factors: race; religion; language or dialect; kinship patterns; nationality; a shared historical past; and some consciousness of kind among members. For study purposes the classification of "Puerto Rican," as in the census, refers to both white and nonwhite individuals who were born in Puerto Rico or had at least one parent born there. "Black" as a category therefore excludes nonwhites of Puerto Rican background. The persons classified as "white" do not comprise an ethnic category, but rather a residual grouping of varied cultural and national backgrounds who are neither "Puerto Rican" nor "Black."

Chart 2. Interviews by Respondent

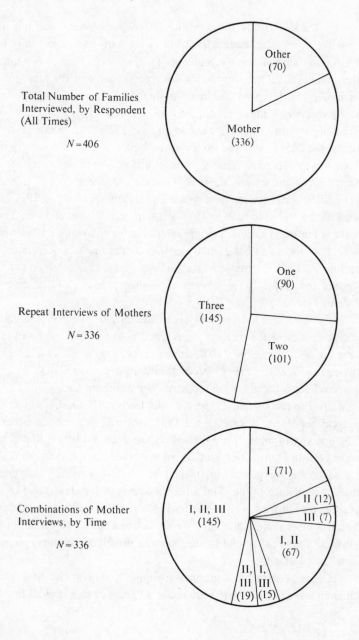

Total Number of Families
Interviewed, by Respondent
(All Times)

$N = 406$

Other
(70)

Mother
(336)

Repeat Interviews of Mothers

$N = 336$

One
(90)

Three
(145)

Two
(101)

Combinations of Mother
Interviews, by Time

$N = 336$

I (71)

II (12)

III (7)

I, II, III
(145)

I, II
(67)

II,
III
(19)

I,
III
(15)

The decision to focus on the 160 mothers interviewed initially and five years later made it possible to measure change not only for the total group but also for each individual mother. There was a question, however, of whether they were representative of the total group of mothers with placed children. An analysis was made for three key study variables—ethnic group, religion, and reason for placement—to see comparability or differences among the 297 initial mother respondents, the 243 interviewed on the second trial, and the 186 seen in the final survey. There were no significant differences in any category; in fact, many figures were identical. Furthermore, there were no significant differences between data on the 26 mothers seen only in 1971 and data on the 160 seen both in 1971 and five years earlier in 1966. Thus there is reason to assume that the sample in the follow-up analysis has several of the same basic characteristics as the mothers seen initially and that, with some cautions, the findings on the change group can be generalized to the larger sample of mothers whose children entered care in 1966.

As background for analysis of the change data, certain stable characteristics of the mothers interviewed both initially and five years later are shown in table 2. The ethnic proportions in the two samples persist: the mothers are 23 percent white, 39 percent Black, and 38 percent Puerto Rican. As to religion, 58 percent are Catholic, 31 percent are Protestant, and 11 percent are Jewish. Of the Catholics, 61 percent are Puerto Rican; of the Protestants, 88 percent are Blacks. The majority of mothers are not native-born New Yorkers—36 percent were born in Puerto Rico and 20 percent were born in the South. As far as reason for placement, mental illness of the mother and emotional disturbance of the child together accounted for almost half of all placements, 26 percent for the former and 18 percent for the latter. The two other major categories are neglect and abuse, 19 percent, and physical illness of the child-caring person, usually the mother, 16 percent.

The women as a group were quite young at the time their children were placed. Half were under 30 years of age, and all but 12

Table 2. *Selected Stable Characteristics of Mothers Interviewed Initially and at Follow-Up (N = 160)*

Characteristics	Percentage Distribution
Ethnic Group:	
Total	100
White	23
Black	39
Puerto Rican	38
Religion:	
Total	100
Catholic	58
Protestant	31
Jewish	11
Birthplace:	
Total	100
New York City	35
Southern United States	20
Other continental United States	4
Puerto Rico	36
Latin America or Europe	5
Age of Mother at Placement:	
Total	100
Under 20	7
20 through 29	42
30 through 39	39
40 or over	12

percent were under 40. On the average, Black women were the youngest in the three ethnic groups, and white women the oldest. The educational level of the study women was considerably below that of the nation as a whole. The average sample mother had completed only 9.3 years of school at the time her children were placed. This compares to a national average for women in 1966 of 11.9 years.[8] Study mothers born in New York City had a higher educational attainment than those born elsewhere, an average of 10.8 years. The women born

[8] U.S. Bureau of the Census, *Current Population Reports, Population Characteristics*, Series P-20, No. 158: 1966 (Washington, D.C., 1966) table 1.

in the South averaged 9.8 years of school and those born in Puerto Rico, 7.1 years. Differences by ethnic group generally reflected those by birthplace. White women had the highest average number of years of schooling (10.5 years), Black women the second highest (10.2 years), and Puerto Rican women the lowest (7.6 years).

During their stay in placement, most of the children of the study families experienced more than one type of foster care, as they moved from temporary to longer-term status. However, for each child it was possible to identify the kind of care received for most of the time in placement. The children of 43 percent of the study mothers spent most of their time in foster homes, living in the community with a family. These children were younger than the average in the sample; their mothers tended to be white or Black rather than Puerto Rican; and they had mainly been placed because of the inability of the mothers to assume care (in the case of newborn infants), family dysfunction, and mental illness of the mother.

Institutional care prevailed for the remainder of the children, with two main types of placement. Children of 11 percent of the mothers were in residential treatment centers. These were youngsters primarily placed because of emotional disturbance and behavioral problems. More than half were white, and the children were older than the sample average. The remaining 46 percent of mothers had children placed in other child-caring institutions. More than half of the women with children in these institutional settings were Puerto Rican, and three-quarters of them were Catholic. The predominant placement reasons for this group were physical illness of the mother, abandonment, neglect and abuse, and inability to continue care.

Basic Study Concepts

Several basic study concepts were developed over the period of investigation, and are employed in the analysis of data. These concepts are set forth below, and will be used throughout the book.

REASONS FOR PLACEMENT

One basic concept used for organizing data on the study sample was the definition of reason for placement. There were numerous problems faced by families at the time of placement; poverty was typically a "necessary" but not "sufficient" condition for foster care. Careful analysis of worker reports, case records, and client interviews made possible the designation of a single "reason for placement" defined not as the major family problem but rather as the key factor resulting in the child's entering care. Eight categories of reason for placement were developed, and these are noted below. The percentage of the follow-up sample that falls into each category is reported.[9]

Mental illness (26 percent). Those cases for which mental illness was judged to be the main reason for placement included two types of situations. The majority involved hospitalization of the mother in a psychiatric facility, often a result of a precipitating episode which indicated that she was a danger to herself or her children. In some cases hospitalization did not occur, but there was a clear indication from the record of emotional disturbances and bizarre behavior.

Child behavior (18 percent). When the main reason for placement was judged to be child behavior, situations existed that indicated emotional disturbance on the part of the placed child. In most cases, professional diagnosis of the child's mental health had been obtained prior to placement. In some cases, no psychiatric diagnosis had been obtained, but the child's behavior had induced the parents to seek help through foster care placement.

Physical illness (14 percent). Judgment of physical illness as the main reason for placement related to the physical incapacity of the mother to care for the child. In most cases, the mother was hospital-

[9] A detailed description of each category, with case illustrations and judgment methodology, appears in Jenkins and Norman, *Filial Deprivation,* chapter 3, "Placement of Children," pp. 53–95. An earlier research study that developed background rationale for the category definitions is Shirley Jenkins and Mignon Sauber, *Paths to Child Placement, Family Situations Prior to Foster Care* (New York: Community Council of Greater New York, Inc., 1966).

ized. In some cases, she remained at home but could not physically undertake child care. A wide range of illnesses was reported.

Inability or unwillingness to assume care (6 percent). Women who had borne out-of-wedlock children and could not, or would not, assume caring for them at the time of birth were placed in this category. These children entered long-term foster care rather than being surrendered for adoption, usually because the mothers hoped eventually to seek return of the child.

Inability or unwillingness to continue care (8 percent). Cases in this category were those in which the child-caring person (usually the mother, but on occasion another individual) could not or would not continue to care for the study child. This differed from the previous category in that there had been prior assumption of responsibility.

Neglect or abuse (19 percent). This category included cases in which the placed child was severely neglected or physically abused. In almost all such cases neighborhood complainants, the Society for the Prevention of Cruelty to Children, the police, or the courts were the initiators of the placement.

Abandonment (2 percent). This category included cases in which the child was placed after desertion by the mother, without any plans for alternate child care.

Family dysfunction (7 percent). Placement for this reason involved serious incapacity on the part of the child-caring person. Included were cases of parental drug addiction, alcoholism, criminal activity, retardation, or serious familial conflict involving violent behavior.

CATEGORY GROUPINGS

Analysis of several key variables and of substantial study data showed statistically significant differences in several areas between two groupings of placement categories. These have been identified as follows:

Socially approved reasons for placement, including physical illness, mental illness, emotional disturbance of the child, and inability or unwillingness to assume care.

Socially unacceptable reasons for placement, including neglect and abuse, unwillingness or inability to continue care, abandonment, or family dysfunction.

SOCIOECONOMIC CIRCUMSTANCES

The index of socioeconomic circumstances was designed to differentiate within the relatively homogeneous study sample, and the variables incorporated reflect characteristics relevant for these particular families. The majority of the study sample experienced one or more situations found in poverty populations, i.e., female-headed households, deteriorated housing, support from public assistance, and lack of an adult working member. Variables utilized in conventional indexes, such as "occupation" and "amount of income," would not have been meaningful for this population.

A socioeconomic index incorporating five appropriate variables was developed.

Variable	*Weight*
Main source of support	3
Education	2
Neighborhood income rank	1
Neighborhood juvenile delinquency rank	1
Number of negative housing conditions	1

Each of the above variables had a different data base, since each reflected a different dimension of socioeconomic status. Data for "main source of support" were based on information about income, dependency, and length of dependent status. Seven intervals were defined. The highest category included self-supporting households with $100 or more in weekly income, and the lowest comprised public welfare households receiving such assistance for six years or more. The variable "education" was based on data reflecting the highest grade completed by the best-educated adult in the child's household.

"Neighborhood income" and "juvenile delinquency" ranks reflected family address, and were computed from comparative data of 74 New York City neighborhoods. Finally, "negative housing conditions" were derived from a list of 20 circumstances considered by authorities to be hazardous to health and safety. Data for this variable were collected by means of interviewer observations of the family living quarters.

The technical tasks of combining these five variables so that each family would have a single score were resolved in the following way. Based on collected data, each family received a preliminary score on each variable. Since there were differences in the range of scores among the different variables, the family score for each was standardized by dividing it by that variable's standard deviation. This resulted in five standardized scores per family.

All the variables utilized were not considered to be of equal importance, and each was therefore assigned a designated weight before they were combined. The weights were based on subjective judgment on the part of the research investigators. "Main source of support" was considered to be the most critical, and was assigned the weight of 3. Education was considered to be next in importance and was assigned a weight of 2. The three variables reflecting neighborhood and housing conditions were each assigned a weight of 1. Finally, each score was multiplied by its own variable's designated weight and the combined weighted scores became the family's socioeconomic score. For use in comparative analysis, the scores of the entire sample were placed on a continuum and evenly divided into three classes, described as high, middle, or low. Families were then so characterized, and the high, middle, or low socioeconomic designation became a critical variable for cross-tabulation with other study data.

Although these three categories differentiate appropriately within the sample, they do not correspond with general population designations of high or low socioeconomic status, and therefore they cannot be compared with findings from other studies without reference to the original data. Used internally in the analysis of this group of families, however, these categories were useful in differentiating circumstances, even within a relatively homogeneous sample.[10]

FILIAL DEPRIVATION

The concept of "filial deprivation" refers to the feelings experienced by natural parents when they are separated from their children. It is the complement of the concept of "maternal deprivation," or the experiences of children separated from their parents. In the family research "filial deprivation" was studied at several points in time: directly after the child entered placement, during the placement, and at the point of discharge from care. The ten major feelings explored were: sad, angry, bitter, relieved, thankful, worried, nervous, guilty, ashamed, and empty. Referents of feelings were also studied, including self, child, other interpersonal, agency, and society.

ATTITUDES: AGENCY AND SOCIAL

The initial interview explored three categories each of parental attitudes to agencies and to society. Agency attitudes were designated as parents' perceiving the agency as a "facilitator" of child care, helping families in times of need; or as a "usurper" of parental rights, taking over child care; or as a "surrogate" for parents, fulfilling a socially appropriate role. General social attitudes included the concept of alienation or anomie, referring to a sense of futility, pessimism, and powerlessness; trust, which is the antithesis of alienation in many ways; and calculativeness, an expression of cynicism and self-interest.

The basic study concepts discussed above will be used in the interpretation of data throughout the book. The report of study findings begins with analysis of the change data, first in circumstances of families, and then in mothers' feelings about placement.

---

[10] For a more detailed statement of the methodology used in developing the index of socioeconomic circumstances, see Jenkins and Norman, *Filial Deprivation,* Appendix, pp. 275–86.

Two

Changes

in

Circumstances

Five years after placement, 73 percent of the children in the follow-up study had been discharged, primarily to the care of their mothers. This reflects a renewed child-caring capacity in the home—but does it also mean that problems leading to placement had been solved? To answer this question the study analyzed the economic position of mothers five years after placement, as compared with their situations at entry; reviewed mobility and living conditions, including housing units and neighborhoods; and noted changes in marital status and household composition. In addition to the quantitative data, case materials were examined to illustrate changes in family situations, some leading to discharge and some prolonging care. The findings show foster care to be a helpful partial program, fulfilling child care needs when parents cannot or will not perform expected roles. Foster care as a program, however, is not part of a fully integrated social welfare system, and thus it is doomed to fail if the expectation is that basic family problems will be solved as a result of placement alone.

Socioeconomic Circumstances

Since the majority of children had returned home five years after placement, the assumption is that the crises that brought them into care had been resolved. The poverty conditions, however, which were a major contributing factor aggravating problems leading to placement, had not changed. The data show that five years after their children's entry into foster care, the economic conditions of mothers had not improved, and in many cases had deteriorated in several respects.

At the time of the original placement in 1966, 45 percent of the 160 mothers in the follow-up study were receiving public assistance as a main source of support, and an additional 3 percent received it as supplementary support. Furthermore, 13 percent of those not receiving public aid had incomes of less than $75 a week. At that time, the typical Aid to Families of Dependent Children monthly payment in New York City for a family of four, including rent allotment, was approximately $257.75, or $3,000 a year.[1] The poverty level for that year for a non-farm family of four established by the United States government was $3,335 annually.[2] Since the number of persons in the average study household was between four and five, it was estimated that the families of at least three out of every five study mothers, or 60 percent, were living at or below the poverty level when their children were placed.

Five years later their situations appeared to have worsened: 58 percent of the same 160 mothers were receiving public assistance as a main source of support, and 13 percent as a supplementary source. An additional 2 percent, not receiving public aid, had incomes of less than

[1] New York City Department of Welfare (presently Department of Social Services), *Basic Department of Welfare Monthly Allowances Effective July 1, 1966* (prepared by Home Economics Program; New York, 1966).

[2] Mollie Orshansky, "The Shape of Poverty in 1966," in *Children's Allowances and the Economic Welfare of Children,* ed. Eveline M. Burns (New York: Citizens Committee for Children of New York, Inc., 1968), p. 21.

$75 a week. The federal poverty level for a non-farm family of four in 1970 had risen by about 20 percent over that of 1966, to $3,968 annually.[3] By that time more than 70 percent of the mothers in the sample had household incomes at or below the poverty level, an increase of 10 percent in five years. Another important change is the rise in the percentage of cases who were receiving some form of public assistance—from 48 percent of mothers in 1966 to 71 percent in 1971.

When the financial position of mothers over the five years is examined, four groups can be identified. These are:

1. 67 mothers who received public assistance at the time of placement and also five years later (42 percent);
2. 47 mothers who did not receive public assistance at placement but did receive it five years later (29 percent);
3. 10 mothers who received public assistance at placement but did not receive it five years later (six percent); and
4. 36 mothers who did not receive public assistance either at placement or five years later (23 percent).

It should be noted that this analysis refers to two points in time, and does not take into account changes that may have occurred during the five years but were reversed by the time of the final follow-up interview. Each of the four categories noted above had some particular characteristics. Mothers receiving welfare both at placement and five years later tended to be older than the others, including 50 percent of mothers forty years or older, 45 percent of those in their thirties, 40 percent of those in their twenties, and 18 percent of the teenagers. In terms of ethnic group, this stable public assistance category included 55 percent of Puerto Rican mothers, 41 percent of Black mothers, and 22 percent of white mothers.

The second category, the 29 percent of mothers who were not on public assistance at placement but were five years later, can be un-

[3] U.S. Bureau of the Census, *Current Population Reports, Consumer Income,* Series P-60, No. 77, May 7, 1971 (Washington, D.C., 1971), table 6.

derstood by reference to both broader social trends and situations specific to the families themselves. The rise in the percentage on public assistance should be placed in context. In 1965 welfare recipiency per 1,000 of the population in New York City was 61.0; by 1971 it had risen to 131.4. More specifically, in the poverty areas welfare recipiency rose by 118 percent during that period.[4] Thus for the study sample, some part of the rise in numbers of mothers on public assistance may reflect this general trend. There was also a substantial increase in number of mothers receiving supplementary assistance, from 3 to 13 percent. This may reflect the inflationary economic situation, which means that many working families could not subsist on earned income alone. The main explanation for the rise, however, lies with a further analysis of the particular situations of the mothers at the time of placement.

Mothers in this category were more likely to have had children placed because of their own physical illness, severe family dysfunction, or abandonment. One-third of this group of women had been hospitalized or institutionalized at the time of placement. Thus although they were not receiving public assistance in 1966, they were in fact being supported by public funds in other sectors of the social service system, such as health and corrections. When they were released from institutions and reentered the community, public assistance was their only immediate source of support. In addition, some other mothers in this category had experienced marital separations during the five years and lost the support of husbands. Finally, some mothers who had been working at the time of placement could no longer do so five years later for health reasons, or because of the birth of a new infant.

The third category of mothers, 6 percent, had been on public assistance at the time of placement but were not five years later. There was a total of 10 women in this group, and in 9 of these cases the

---

[4] Abraham C. Burstein, *New York City Community Corporation Areas* (City of New York Human Resources Administration, Office of Public Affairs, March 1972), p. 46.

placement of the child in foster care had freed the mothers to seek employment. These women were working and self-supporting at the time of the final field interview, but their children remained in care.

The last category, mothers who were not on public assistance either at placement or five years later, had a high representation of white mothers, 51 percent, as compared with 16 percent and 12 percent for Black and Puerto Rican women, respectively. Many were families where placement had occurred because of the emotional disturbance of the children. These families were usually of a relatively higher income status than others in the study, and acute poverty did not figure prominently in the household situations.

This review of change data on economic circumstances of study families illustrates the problem of looking at only one aspect of the social service system to evaluate outcome. Are things worse because more mothers are on public assistance five years after placement? Not, as the data show, if many of the mothers were in hospitals or institutions when children entered care. Similarly, the fact that some mothers who had been on public assistance at placement were working five years later is not an unqualifiedly successful outcome, since their children remained in foster care. In any study of change, the investigation considers the input factors, the output factors, and factors that remain stable, the ''stay-put'' factors. In this case it is the ''stay-put'' that predominate. For 65 percent of mothers, there was in fact no change in source of support over the five years of the study.

Living Conditions

Poverty status, poor neighborhoods, and deteriorated living conditions tend to go together. At the time of placement, two-thirds of the households in the study were located in the 20 ''poverty'' neighborhoods of New York City. These 20 neighborhoods had the highest juvenile delinquency rates and the lowest median family incomes of all New

York City neighborhoods.[5] In addition, the dwelling units of these families had large numbers of highly negative housing conditions such as rats, roaches, rotting apartment floors, and garbage littering the building halls.[6]

To determine the relative neighborhood conditions of families five years later, account had to be taken not only of movement of families but also of changes in neighborhood ranks for both income and juvenile delinquency. The original rankings had been based on 1960 population data, which were out of date by the time of the study follow-up in 1971. Furthermore, shifts in boundary designations of community districts over ten years resulted in a base of 62 neighborhoods, rather than the 74 utilized in the earlier study based on 1960 data.

A new analysis of study families was made based on 1970 data, and the earlier neighborhood designations were recomputed. It was decided to use median family income as the criterion of neighborhood level, since this correlated most highly with a series of other socioeconomic variables. New 1965 estimates were made by averaging 1960 and 1970 data for all neighborhoods and then ranking them. New rank scores were assigned to all 160 families. The rankings based on 1970 data alone were also made, and each family thus had two neighborhood rank scores, one based on their 1966 address and a comparable score based on their 1971 address. This procedure thus

[5] For the initial study, New York City neighborhoods were ranked according to median family income and juvenile delinquency rates from 1960 data. The highest- and lowest-ranking neighborhoods had median family incomes of $9,700 and $3,700 per year, respectively, and juvenile delinquency rates of 8 delinquents per 1,000 youths and 101 per 1,000, respectively. See Shirley Jenkins, *Comparative Recreation Needs and Services in New York Neighborhoods* (New York: Community Council of Greater New York, Inc., Research Department, 1963), pp. 33–37.

[6] After a review of standards for dwellings and consultations with housing specialists, a list of 21 items reflecting conditions dangerous to health and safety was prepared. The data on dwelling units where sample children lived at the time of placement were based on observations of staff interviewers and reports of family members. See Shirley Jenkins and Elaine Norman, *Filial Deprivation and Foster Care* (New York: Columbia University Press, 1972), pp. 32–33.

allowed both moves by families and shifts in neighborhood ranks to be taken into account.

To secure an overall picture of change, the 1965 and 1970 ranks of neighborhoods were compared for two variables in the original index of socioeconomic circumstances. As would be expected, neighborhoods in New York City do not change much in relative standing over five years. The rank correlation of 62 neighborhoods on median family income for 1965 and 1970 was .99. For juvenile delinquency the rank correlation for the same years was almost as high, .95. Thus changes noted for families were primarily attributable to their own moves rather than to improvement or deterioration in the same neighborhood in terms of the criteria used.

Although there was little movement in neighborhood ranks, there was substantial movement of families within neighborhoods, among neighborhoods, and among boroughs. After five years, 81 percent of the mothers in the follow-up study were living at different addresses than they had been when the children entered placement. Of the 160 families, only 31 (19 percent) did not move; 39 (24 percent) moved to another address in the same neighborhood; 43 (27 percent) moved to another neighborhood in the same borough; and 36 (23 percent) moved to another borough in the city. There were 11 families (7 percent) in the follow-up study with no home city address, these mothers having been reinterviewed either out of town or in institutions.

These data show substantial changes in housing for the study sample, far in excess of those for the total population. For New York City as a whole, 59 percent of the population five years old and over were at the same address in 1970 as in 1965, as compared with only 19 percent of the study mothers. (Conversely, 41 percent of the city's population changed addresses in five years, as compared with 81 percent of the study families.) [7] When families did move, however, the

[7] U.S. Bureau of the Census, *General Social and Economic Characteristics: New York,* "Mobility, Commuting, and Veteran Status, for Areas and Places: 1970" (Washington, D.C., 1970) table 82.

direction of movement did not differ substantially from that of the study sample. For the city as a whole, 61 percent of those who moved stayed in the same borough; the corresponding figure for the study sample was 58 percent.

When the direction of movement is examined for the study sample, it can be seen that the highest percentage of movement where boroughs changed was out of Manhattan. Of 48 families who lived in Manhattan at the time of the initial interview, 38 moved, 17 of these moving to another borough. Their movement was in the same direction as that in the city as a whole. As noted, 61 percent of those who moved in New York stayed in the same borough; this was true for only 49 percent of Manhattan residents.

Where did sample families move when they made major changes in their residences? Of the 36 mothers who changed boroughs, 13 went to Brooklyn, 11 to the Bronx, 5 each to Manhattan and Queens, and 2 to Richmond. This meant a shift in borough concentration to Brooklyn and the Bronx, with Manhattan dropping from first to third place as the residence of families five years after placement. This geographical shift is relevant to the analysis of changes in neighborhood rankings for study families.

With a mobility rate of 81 percent, there are sufficient data to see if families improved their circumstances by all the changes in housing. The criterion was whether they moved to a higher- or lower-income neighborhood. In spite of the apparent worsening of economic circumstances of the families, there is evidence of some improvement in the level of income in the neighborhoods where they live. With 62 neighborhoods in the ranking scheme, it was arbitrarily decided to define "no change" as any move within plus or minus three rank steps. This accounted for 84 of the 149 families with 1970 city addresses, or 56 percent. Thus there was no change in neighborhood levels for 90 percent of families who did not move, and for 47 percent of those who did move.

Neighborhood levels worsened for 22 families, or 15 percent, and they improved for 43 families, or 29 percent. Both groups can be broken down into two categories, first those who were "somewhat" worse and "somewhat" better off, with movement from 4 to 14 ranks. This included movement by 10 percent of the families to poorer neighborhoods, and 13 percent to slightly higher-income neighborhoods. The second category included the 5 percent of families who were in much poorer neighborhoods, over 15 ranks lower, and the 15 percent of families in neighborhoods over 15 ranks higher in income.

Although the numbers are small, some of the improvement in neighborhood rank can be traced to the movement from Manhattan: 17 families left that borough, 9 to better neighborhoods. Of these, 6 went to Brooklyn, 1 to the Bronx, and 2 to Queens. Of the families who moved to substantially higher-income neighborhoods, nearly half were Puerto Rican; approximately one-quarter each were Blacks and whites, respectively. In terms of negative housing conditions, however, Puerto Rican families who moved were most likely to be in more deteriorated housing than they had been in before the change. And in spite of all the movement, affecting 81 percent of mothers, over half or 56 percent were in neighborhoods of the same economic level five years after placement, whether at the same or a new address.

Family Life

Contributing to the placement of children is the fact that frequently there is only one parent in the home to carry the total responsibility of care. As a result, illness or breakdown of the adult leaves children without a functioning caretaker. At the time of their children's entry into care only 20 percent of the 160 women in the follow-up study were married and living with their spouses.[8] An additional 34 percent were married but separated from their husbands; 10 percent were divorced or widowed, and 36 percent had never married.

---

[8] The 20 percent included 15 percent whose spouses were biological fathers of the children in care, and 5 percent whose spouses were not fathers of these children.

These data on marital status may in fact overstate the percentage of legally married respondents, because the information was derived from self-reports from the mothers. Since there was no way, without violation of the study limits of confidentiality and privacy, to verify the legal marital status, the study data report information given verbally by mothers to social work interviewers. The response that they were "married" could therefore encompass both legal and common-law relationships.

Five years after placement the marital status of over two-thirds of the mothers remained the same. In particular, four-fifths of mothers who were divorced or widowed when children entered care retained that status five years later. The women who were married at placement and remained so five years later were most likely to be older, Jewish, white, and not dependent on public assistance at any time during the study period. Placement in these cases often occurred because of the child's emotional or behavior problems, and the child was usually placed in a residential treatment center. Mothers who were single and remained so five years later were most likely to be young, Black or Puerto Rican, and receiving public assistance both at the time of placement and at the time of follow-up. Women who were divorced or widowed throughout the study period tended to be older on the average and also to have been receiving public assistance on a continuous basis.

The number of women who changed from one marital status to another during the five-year study period was relatively small, fewer than one-third of the total. Twenty women who were previously single had married during the study period, but by the time of the last interview 12 of them were separated from their new husbands. Separation rather than divorce occurred for all 10 women who were married and living with their spouses at the time of placement but not five years later. Nine women who were separated at placement were subsequently divorced, whereas 7 others who were separated reconciled with their spouses. Finally, 3 divorced or widowed women remarried over the five years.

The major shift in household composition over the study period was in the higher percentage of mothers living alone five years after placement. This resulted primarily from the movement to their own households of mothers who had been hospitalized or institutionalized when children entered care (20 percent). Thus after five years 21 percent of mothers lived alone, as compared with 5 percent at placement. The percentage of mothers living with children only was the same, 35 percent, at both times. The percentage living with spouse, with or without children, rose slightly from 20 to 27 percent. The fact that some children remained in care resulted in the reversal in figures for mothers living with other adults only, or other adults and children. At placement the former category was only 4 percent, rising to 12 percent five years later, whereas the latter category included 14 percent at placement but only 5 percent five years later. The pattern discerned from the changes in household composition tends to be that households of women and children or couples with children remain the same, but the percentage of households of single women rises, as does that of adults only, when children remain in care.

Discharge of Children

Clearly the major change over the five years was the discharge of children from foster care. At the time of the last follow-up interview, 73 percent of the 160 children were out of placement, primarily being discharged to the home of the mother. Twenty-six children had been discharged to other relatives, primarily to their fathers, grandparents, or aunts. The amount of time children remained in care varied considerably for the different categories of reason for placement. But there were other important factors, such as changes in the mother's condition, newly volunteered support from family or friends, and help from community and social agencies. The determination of the mother to have her child home was also a key ingredient in the discharge process.

The high percentage of children returned home in five years cannot be generalized to the entire foster care population. The follow-up study reported here was based on a sample of mothers interviewed three times over five years, and thus they tend to represent a more stable and accessible group than the cases interviewed initially but not found later. Even within the study sample, however, it is possible to identify factors associated with length of stay in care.

At the halfway point. At the time of the second field interview, two and one-half years after placement, 54 percent of children in the study sample were still in care, and 46 percent had been discharged. An analysis was made of the relationship of problem solution to discharge status. In the field interview, mothers were reminded of what they had stated, at the time of placement, to be the main problem leading to the child going into care. They were then asked whether they thought that problem had been solved or still existed. Discharge status was also noted.

Four groups were identified, based on respondent reports:

1. Problem persists, child remains in care.
2. Problem persists, child discharged.
3. Problem resolved, child remains in care.
4. Problem resolved, child discharged.

Of particular interest are categories 2 and 3. In the cases in which respondents felt the problem continued, but children had been discharged, a significantly higher percentage of families were white, were married and included spouses, had a salaried income, and were in the ''high'' rank in socioeconomic status. Mothers in this group visited their children more frequently (over once a month) than did mothers in any of the other groups.

The families in which mothers said the placement problem had been solved but the child remained in foster care had significantly different characteristics. Over half of these families were Black—a higher proportion than in any other category. Nearly half of the respondents were divorced or separated and nearly a third were single. The percentage of mothers married and living with their husbands was lower for this group than for any other. Over half of the respondents and nearly two-thirds of the mothers in this group were supported by public assistance—the highest percentages in any category—despite the fact that the study children were still in placement. More of these families fell into the lowest socioeconomic rank than did those in any other group. Mothers in this category visited their children less regularly than did those in other groups.

The mothers' statements on whether or not problems were solved cannot be taken as more than their own perceptions of the situation. Workers who interviewed families were also asked to make judgments, however, and they agreed with mothers to about the same extent in both categories—those who claimed resolution and those who said problems persisted. The strength of the socioeconomic variables seems to persist in discharge as well as in placement. Single-parent families and welfare status appear for these families to be related to the potential for discharge, and placement is hardly likely to have affected either of those variables.

Five years later. By five years after placement, when the majority of children were home, a further analysis was made to identify variables associated with leaving placement. Factors related to the initial entry into care were reviewed to see if they were related to the discharge process.

The average amount of time the children had remained in care prior to discharge varied considerably for the different placement reasons. They seemed to fall in three groups. The average (median) time in care for discharged children placed because of physical illness of the mother or her inability to assume care was under one year, or 10.5 and 11.9 months, respectively. Two placement reasons, mental illness of the mother and neglect and abuse of the child, kept discharged children in care about one and one-half years, or 16.7 months for each. Longest time in care for discharged children, over two years, was for those placed for child behavior, 26.9 months; severe family dysfunction, 26 months; and inability of families to continue care, 24.4 months.

The figures on time in care of discharged children do not reflect the categories of children who remain in care longer than the five-year study period. For example, child behavior cases tended to stay in care for an average of two years, probably reflecting the course of treatment, but 83 percent of all such cases went home within five years. The average time before discharge for neglect and abuse and mental illness cases was only 16.7 months, yet only 63 and 64 percent of these categories of children, respectively, went home within five years. Although the numbers in each category are too small for generalization, it is suggested that length of time in care for children placed for these reasons may follow a bimodal distribution, with early return home for those who return and long-term stay for others.

CASE ILLUSTRATIONS

Although it was possible to identify a major "reason for placement," problems were by no means unidimensional. Discharge was also a complicated procedure, some but not all needs having been met. Case illustrations for each of the placement categories point up the complexities of the discharge situations, as well as conditions which meant children remained in care.

Child behavior. This was the only category in which the child was identified as the focus of the placement decision, but even in these cases there were many complicating family factors. Separation of child from family in many cases allowed time for working out of problems, particularly if the child was in a residential treatment center and services to families were also provided. Such supportive psychiatric and counseling services were utilized by two-thirds of the mothers whose children entered care for this reason. The case illustration cited here points up changes occurring for one family over the study period.

Case #355 (Discharged): A typical child behavior case is that of Mrs. J., a white, Jewish woman, 44 years old at the time her 10-year old son was placed because of "odd" hyperactive behavior. Neither his mother nor his teachers could cope with him. "He knew no limits," said Mrs. J. "He was a danger to himself and to others." The child's father traveled a great deal and was rarely home. He thought that the child's main problem was that "he was spoiled" and he "fought the placement every inch of the way." There was a great deal of marital conflict in the home. According to Mrs. J., Mr. J. drank a lot, abused her continually, and beat her occasionally. "I am his victim," she stated. The child remained in residential treatment for two and one-half years during which time he "developed into a beautiful, normal boy," said his mother at the first follow-up interview. During that time, the mother received psychiatric help and apparently developed a greater understanding of her relationship with her child. "I don't think it's my son's problem as much as mine," she said. "I always took my anger out on my children [there was also an older son, no longer living at home], and not on [its real source] their father." While the child was in placement Mrs. J., with much relief, separated from her husband. Her source of support became public assistance.

At the final follow-up interview held two and one-half years after the discharge, the family situation did not seem to be quite as positive. The boy was "slipping downhill again," playing hooky and acting out destructively once more. He was being served by Big Brothers but seemed to be continually testing his surrogate "brother" by burdensome demands for attention and continual phone calls "at all hours of the day and night." Although the placement agency provided for after-care treatment for the boy, he was not meeting his appointments. The mother-child relationship also seemed to have deteriorated. At the end of the last study interview, the social worker interviewer noted, "mother and son carry on like peers. Very adolescent behavior displayed by both."

Case #331 (*In care*): The 39-year-old mother in this case is an American Indian woman whose husband was Black. The mother stated that discrimination was one of the factors which affected their personal relationship, and they were separated at the time of the first interview. The child's difficulties in school had led to his placement. According to the mother, he was a bright boy who was bored and so walked around the room. The father, however, felt he had "lost control" of the child, who was rebellious, in bad company, and would just "clam up" and not communicate. The mother felt that placement had helped her son. At the second interview she said the child was best off in placement because of the "situation in the cities in general—he could get in trouble here." As a working mother, she felt he would get better supervision in an institution than "out in the streets." Five years later she felt the same way, saying "He has gotten more things from the institution than he could have gotten from a poor family." She sees the boy each Sunday, when he comes home, and says he "has grown and developed."

Physical illness. Cases in which children were placed because of physical illness of the child-caring person tended to be less complicated, with children staying in care less than a year on the average, and with 86 percent having been discharged during the five-year study period. The severity of the mother's illness was related to time in care, with tuberculosis, stroke, and cerebral palsy being among the diagnoses that meant extended child placement. The discharge of children was made possible when mothers recovered. Supplementary help was sometimes needed, particularly if the family home had been disbanded. In these cases, availability of public assistance, help in finding new apartments, homemaker services, and help from family members were all factors in creating the circumstances in which children could return home. In cases for which only medical help was needed, however, child discharge was a relatively routine procedure.

Case #023   (Discharged): Miss R. is an unmarried Black mother supported by public assistance since the birth of her first child. She was 24 years old at the time her three infant children were placed. Miss R. required emergency hospitalization for jaundice and hepatitis, and the Department of Social Services arranged for temporary placement in a foster home. Miss R. was hospitalized for a month. The children were returned to her home several months later when she was able to care for them. She felt that the children had been well cared for and were "healthy and happy." She was grateful for the placement, as it allowed her to regain her health and strength. During the four and one-half years between the discharge and the final study interview, the major change in Miss R.'s life was the addition to her family of three more children, born approximately a year and one-half apart. Five years after the initial placement, at the age of 29, she was maintaining her home, still on public assistance, and caring for her six young children.

Case #032   (In care): Mrs. R. is a Black mother of 25 whose child was placed because she had active tuberculosis, the father was in jail, and her family wouldn't help. She resented the placement saying "I was trying to be a good mother and signed myself out of the hospital so I could take care of my child, but they took him saying I would contaminate him." By the second interview, two and one-half years later, the mother said her TB was arrested, but she stays sick all the time. She reported she knew nothing about where her child was. At that time the interviewer reported that Mrs. R. appeared disturbed, rambled in conversation, and that her apartment was "a complete mess, filthy, filled with junk."

At the final field interview, Mrs. R.'s health appeared improved, the TB was arrested, but the child continued in care. She had not seen him in five years. She said, "No one tells me anything." The father was also seen. He said the child had been placed for his own protection. He saw him once four years ago. He said he would like to get him back but doesn't know to whom to talk—the welfare people or the health people. The interviewer commented that the father kept dropping off and nodding, seeming to be either on drugs or alcohol. He had no regular income and just "made out." It was apparent that the initial placement reason, TB, had been superseded by the overall family disorganization.

Unable or unwilling to assume care. Among the women who did not care for their infants after birth, 9 were unmarried; and in the tenth case the legal husband was not the father of the baby. Although they did not assume care, none of these mothers wanted to surrender their infants for adoption. In under a year, 8 of the 10 had their babies home with them. By the time of the follow-up interview, half had given birth to another child.

Case #297 (Discharged): This 18-year-old Black unwed mother wanted to "finish high school and get a good job" and planned the placement before the child was born. The maternal grandmother was unable to take the child due to crowded home conditions. The child was placed, over the objections of the father. By the time of the second interview the mother had finished school, gotten a job at a bank, saved some money, and then taken the child home to the maternal grandmother, who cared for the child while the mother worked. This was still the situation at the final interview, five years after placement.

Case #007 (In care): This mother, a white Catholic woman, had nine in-wedlock children. She had conceived the placed child by a man other than her husband and was ashamed of that as well as that the man was "Spanish." She was concerned about the skin color of the child, since the father was "very dark.'' At the time of the original placement, she had rejected the idea of adoption for that child. Five years later she had changed her mind and was seriously considering surrender. By then she had separated from her husband, was on public assistance, and had placed four of her other nine children in foster care.

Mental illness. In about two-thirds of the cases in this category, mothers were hospitalized because of mental illness; in the remainder of cases mothers were diagnosed and symptoms reported, and outpatient counseling or treatment was provided. Discharge of children occurred at approximately the same rate whether or not mothers were hospitalized in mental institutions.

Case #397   (Discharged): Mrs. R. is a Puerto Rican, Catholic, 24-year-old mother of three who was deserted by the children's father. Her Department of Social Services worker suggested she visit an outpatient clinic at Metropolitan Hospital when she complained of being depressed and nervous. She said she hit the children for the slightest thing. Afraid that she might lose control and hurt her children, she made arrangements to have the children placed. They were still in placement two years later. Mrs. R. continued in treatment, went to work and began living with a new common-law husband with whom she shortly had a child. By the time of the last study interview, five years after entry, the placed children were discharged home. Mrs. R. said, ''I learned I couldn't live without the kids.''

Case #143   (Discharged—in care): Mrs. T. is a 40-year-old white, Jewish mother, separated from her addicted husband after a stormy marriage, overwhelmed by depression and unable at the time of placement to care for her four children. She was not able to send them off to school. Previous to the placement there was a homemaker in the home for almost two years. Mrs. T. had been hospitalized and in treatment in the past, although she was not hospitalized at the time of placement and during the five-year study period. She did, however, continue to receive psychiatric care. She said her family thought she was a ''bad mother'' for placing the children, but she thinks she ''did them a favor.'' Five years after the placement, three of her children were home. One remained in care, and she felt he was doing well, improving in school, and getting advantages like medical care, music lessons, and camp. Mrs. R. is visited weekly by the placement agency social worker and is more optimistic about the future. She has gotten better housing, which had been a severe problem for her.

Case #392   (Discharged): Mrs. P., a 21-year-old Puerto Rican mother, told the interviewer, "I tried to commit suicide and I was put in a mental hospital for three or four months. I left the kids with my girlfriends but they were only 15 and 16 and didn't do a good job. When my husband found out, he placed them in foster care. He did that to get back at me because he could have called my mother." This was the second suicide attempt for Mrs. P. in two years, and the second hospitalization.

By the time of the third interview five years later, Mrs. P. was home, caring for her children. She reported that she had divorced her husband and was happily remarried. She felt her children had been mistreated in foster care, being severely punished, hit, and isolated. Mrs. P. completed the sentence in the interview instrument, "For a mother a child is ———." with the words, "joy, torture, and suffering."

Neglect and abuse. This group included cases of child beating and other serious physical abuse; sexual molestation; severe malnutrition; and cases in which young children were left alone, and unattended, often and for long periods of time. In almost all instances, the neglect or abuse of the child came to the attention of the police or other social agency through a complaint by a neighbor or other observing party. Often the mother did not recognize the harm to the child involved and considered the placement agency a usurper of parental rights. Despite the severity of most of the parental actions precipitating placement, as noted, 63 percent of these children were discharged from care within five years, with the average time in placement for the discharged children being 16.7 months.

In two cases in which there was sexual abuse of children by unrelated men in the household, mothers separated from the men who had committed the offenses, and the children were discharged home. For the other cases, however, the follow-up interviews did not reveal substantial differences in family patterns or attitudes toward child-rearing between cases in which children had been discharged and cases where they were still in care. In physical abuse cases, and in cases of inadequate supervision, the percentage discharged was equal to the percentage remaining in care—the offense was apparently unrelated to discharge status. What was important, however, was whether or not mothers actively agitated for the return of their children. The mothers who conducted active campaigns to "get my children back" had apparently been successful, whereas those who showed a passive, sometimes willing, acceptance of the placement had children who remained in care. Maternal aggressiveness in this regard appeared to be more related to discharge than was family pathology or therapeutic outcome.

Case #012   (Discharged): Miss K. is a 42-year-old, Black, Protestant, unmarried mother of five children. Miss K. had a drinking problem and apparently often left the children alone. She stated that the placement was due to her drinking and "neglect" of the children. She said that an aunt who lived next door called the police "to scare me." "I was out drinking and having a good time when I should have been home with the children." After the placement, Miss K. noted, "The only thing on my mind was to get my children back. I had to prove myself [to the court probation officer]." She stopped drinking, and within a year her children were discharged home. At the time of the last study interview, four years after the discharge, she had not gone back to drinking. "The placement," she said, "made me a better mother. It taught me a lesson. It really straightened me out."

Case #073   (In care): Miss P., a Puerto Rican, 23-year-old mother of three children, whose father was in jail at the time, said that placement had occurred because of her physical neglect of the children. She told the interviewer, "The children were sick and had to be put in the hospital. They had a rash all over their bodies. The welfare investigator told me it would be best to put them someplace until they were older. He didn't say anything else. I didn't question it; I was afraid to lose my check." By the time of the second interview, the children's father, who was an addict, had died. Three children were still in care, but the mother had a new baby. Miss P.'s unquestioning, passive attitude persisted throughout the final interview. Five years after entry, the children were still in foster care, and she said, "I have no complaints." She does not visit her children because, "I do not know how to travel by subway. I don't speak the language."

Inability or unwillingness to continue care. Of the 14 children placed for this reason, 10 were discharged within five years of the original placement. In all 10 cases, the life circumstances of the mothers had changed so as to facilitate the return of the child. In 3 of these cases, the women had either reunited with their former husbands or begun living with a new spouse, a situation that stabilized their lives considerably. In 4 other cases, young mothers had placed their children in order to "get back on my feet." This meant finishing school, continuing employment, finding their own apartments. Each of these 4 women became pregnant again. With the birth of the second child, they began receiving public assistance and requested the return of the first child. In all instances in which the children remained in care (4 children in 3 families) the original placement had occurred because of the mother's inability to cope with the child's situation rather than their own. One child had tuberculosis, another had bleeding ulcers, the third was addicted, and the fourth was slightly retarded. Five years after placement, these four children were still in care.

Case #193 (*Discharged*): Miss K. is a 19-year-old Black, Catholic, unwed mother who has been living with her own mother at the time of placement. Her baby has colic, and his constant crying aggravated the already serious conflict in the home between Miss K. and her mother. The young woman secured placement for the child so as to escape a difficult home situation. After the placement, Miss K. moved out of her mother's home, got her own apartment, went to school, and eventually obtained a job. Sometime later, however, she became pregnant. She had to leave her job with the birth of the second child. By the time of the final study interview she was receiving public assistance, and had secured the discharge of her first child. When asked what would have helped her, she said, "not having babies at such an early age."

Family dysfunction. Cases were placed in this category for widely varied reasons, including drug addiction, incarceration, alcoholism, retardation and intense family conflict. Discharge patterns did not vary with the specific placement reason, but did appear to reflect receipt of counseling help. Although the numbers were too few to generalize, it should be noted that 5 of the 7 mothers whose children were discharged in the five years after placement had had some type of counseling or therapy while they were in care, whereas only one mother of the four nondischarged children had received such help.

Case #182 (*In care*): Mrs. B. is a 44-year-old Black, Catholic woman, with a drinking problem. She often left her children alone for days at a time. Her husband had to work and could not care for them regularly. While Mrs. B. was on a "drinking spree," Mr. B. placed the children. By the time of the third interview, the couple had divorced. Mrs. B. was receiving public assistance and living with another man. The interviewer felt her condition to have deteriorated from the alcohol; she could not leave the house without help. She was not in contact with any of her children. However, the children's father had remarried and was working. He stated that he intended to take his children out of placement as soon as he found a large enough apartment. He expressed great interest in and concern for the children, and visited them regularly.

Case #046 (Discharged): The children of this 28-year-old Black Catholic mother were placed while she served a short jail sentence for "running numbers." She blames her husband for placing the children. The father's story was different. He said the mother was with another man and he had been paying someone to care for the children and couldn't afford it anymore. The children were discharged to the mother after three years in care. She had gotten out of jail, divorced her husband, remarried, and received "help in getting back" at a mental health clinic. She spoke warmly of the support and interest of the social worker.

REENTRY

For some children, discharge was a revolving door. In 17 cases, they left and reentered care within the study period, in 10 of these for the same reason as the original placement. The primary reasons for placement in the reentry groups were physical illness and neglect and abuse, and the children were Black and Puerto Rican rather than white.

In reviewing the data, the major discernible difference between entry and reentry was in the mothers' perceptions of the necessity of placement. At the initial phase, only 12 percent of these women felt placement was absolutely necesssary, whereas at reentry 41 percent said placement was absolutely necessary and 18 percent said that it was very necessary. Since there were few changes in family circumstances, and most mothers said children entered care at both times for the same reasons, it can only be concluded that the experience of having had children in care turned the mothers' attitudes toward placement in a more favorable direction. For example, one mother who was mentally ill and could not care for her children commented on their re-entry to care, "I feel sad, but at least this time I know from experience that I can get them back."

Summary

What changes occur in five years for families unable to cope with child care? For one thing, the poor got poorer, or at least a higher percentage were dependent on public assistance. For another, in spite of their child-caring problems, they continued to have children. They moved a great deal; four out of five mothers were at different addresses after five years. In the moves, although most families stayed in neighborhoods of the same income level, more families improved their neighborhood circumstances than worsened them—some by moving out of the low-income Manhattan areas. Marital status did not change appreciably for the majority of the group, although there were many shifts in status. Where there were marital breakups, separation rather than divorce tended to occur. For the children, however, the instability in alliances and many shifts in relationships exposed them to new adults, and new adjustments. More women were living alone five years after placement, primarily those who had been institutionalized or hospitalized at the time of entry.

Factors relating to discharge, as well as to remaining in care, are revealing of the problems of these families. At midpoint in the study, two and one-half years after entry, for families in which parents felt the problem was solved but the children remained in care and for those in which the problem persisted but children were home, single-parent status and public assistance tended to mitigate against discharge, while an intact family and self-support favored it.

One problem in a follow-up study is deciding whether problems seen at a later date are old ones persisting or new ones developing. Depending on this decision, the foster placement might be evaluated as a success or a failure. For example, the 10-year-old who was placed in a residential treatment center, spent two years there, and was functioning well at age 12 was having problems at age 15. It could have been predicted that adolescence and the separation of his parents would create new problems for him, and the placement would not necessarily have prepared him for the new situation. In a different case, an unwed mother in her twenties who got sick placed three young children. Five years later, still in her twenties, she had had three more babies, for a total of six. Another bout of illness could only result in another placement, this time of twice as many children.

In numerous cases it was shown that solutions in one area led to problems in other areas. There were cases where mothers reported relief at separation from spouses, after extensive marital discord. However, dependence on public assistance soon followed. Cases in which mothers reported going off public assistance and being self-supporting often meant that children remained in placement, since there were no feasible alternatives for child care.

Although undoubtedly preventive and community services could have made it possible for a percentage of these children to remain at home, the review of the changes in family circumstances over five years tends to support the need for foster care as an institution that can take total responsibility for children during a period of parental incapacity and severe family crisis. It is, however, a partial service, not effective in preventing further placement or resolving the problems that brought children into care. All the evidence points to the need for an integrated family and child welfare system.

Three

Filial Deprivation over Time

Filial deprivation, or separation experiences of parents when children enter care, was a major theme in the analysis of the initial interviews in the family study. This experience, which had not been previously explicated or systematically studied, is an aspect of the placement transaction reciprocal to maternal deprivation, which has indeed been subject to major research investigation. In a society in which the nuclear family is held to be ideal, and the prevailing expectation is that parents will raise their own progeny, child placement is likely to be regarded by the public as at the worst, unnatural, and at the best, undesirable. This can have serious consequences for biological parents as well as for their children. How parents feel about separation, and how these feelings are related to the placement experience, are important dimensions for study. They have implications both for working with parents while children are in care and for facilitating the reentry process.

To secure data on one aspect of how mothers felt about having a child in placement, a checklist of 10 key feeling words had been incorporated in the first interview instrument. The list was developed after extensive preliminary interviewing with parents separated from children. The words were: sad, worried, nervous, empty, angry, bitter, thankful, relieved, guilty, and ashamed. Two additional words, numb and paralyzed, were included in the initial field interview but later dropped because of limited response.

The analysis of the first field interview revealed complicated constellations of feelings, which were associated with some of the key study variables. Feelings were particularly related to reason for placement, alienation of parents, and parents' perceptions of the necessity of placement. There was little difference in the pattern of feelings expressed by mothers and fathers regarding placement when both parents of the same child were interviewed separately. Referents of feelings were also explored, and here definite patterns were found to exist in terms of whether a feeling was primarily referred, for example, to oneself, to the child, to another related adult (primarily the spouse), to the agency, or to society as a whole. Although parents seemed to be showing ambivalence in reporting feelings, they were not so much stating contradictions or confusion as expressing the complicated combinations of feelings that did in fact coexist. A parent could often be sad, angry, nervous, and worried, all at the same time.[1]

The longitudinal nature of the family study, with repeat interviews over five years, provided the opportunity in the follow-up to secure answers to a number of key research questions, such as:

1. Do feelings about placement persist over time?
2. Do these feelings consistently have the same referents?
3. If changes in feelings occur, what is their direction and with what characteristics are such changes associated?

[1] For a detailed analysis of the feelings expressed at the time of the initial interview, see Jenkins and Norman, *Filial Deprivation and Foster Care* (New York: Columbia University Press, 1972), chapter 4, "Feeling Dimensions and Referents in Filial Deprivation Experiences," pp. 97–140.

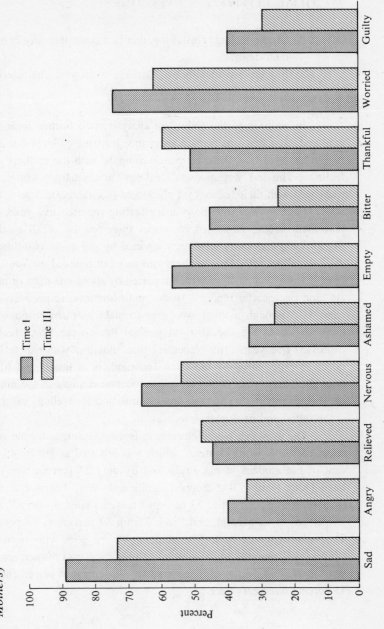

Chart 3. Expression and Persistence of Feelings over Five Years About Having a Child in Foster Care (N = 160 Mothers)

4. Do the feelings cluster together in a consistent way in repeat interviews?
5. If there are identifiable clusters, with what characteristics are these associated?

In addition to the follow-up analysis, two further areas were explored. The first was how mothers thought their children felt about placement, and how these estimates compare with the mothers' own feelings. The last was mothers' feelings on discharge, which were compared with their feelings on placement (see table 3).

Sadness was still the primary feeling reported five years after placement, being expressed by about three-fourths of all mothers; thankfulness and worry were each reported by just under two-thirds of mothers; about half of the mothers said they felt relieved, nervous, and empty; anger and guilt were each reported by about one-third of mothers; and one-quarter reported shame and bitterness, respectively (see chart 3). Although mothers were free to make as many responses as they wished to the checklist, in general there were fewer feelings expressed five years after placement than initially, with 680 feelings noted as experienced by the same 160 mothers at time I and 610 at time III. There were, however, only moderate changes in the ranking of feelings reported. The rank-order correlation for feelings expressed at the initial and final interviews was .86.

The most substantial changes in feeling responses for the group occurred to the word "bitter," which was reported as felt by 45 percent of the mothers at placement and by only 24 percent five years later. Other feelings that dropped significantly were "nervous," from 67 percent at placement to 53 percent five years later, "worry," from 74 percent to 62 percent, and "sad," from 89 percent to 74 percent. The only increases in feeling responses were seen with regard to "thankful," reported by 51 percent at placement and 59 percent five years later, and "relieved," reported by 44 percent at placement and 48 percent five years later.

Table 3. Percentage of Mothers Expressing Feelings Experienced By Themselves on Placement and Discharge, and by Children on Placement

| | Mothers' Own Feelings | | | |
| | On Placement (N = 160) | | On Discharge (N = 110) | Mothers' Estimates of Childrens' Feelings (N = 160) |
Feeling	At Time of Entry	Five Years Later		
Sad	89	74	8	49
Angry	40	34	7	27
Relieved	44	48	68	21
Nervous	67	53	33	38
Ashamed	33	25	4	12
Empty	57	50	1	23
Bitter	45	24	8	21
Thankful	51	59	83	26
Worried	74	62	28	41
Guilty	39	34	11	7

Perhaps one of the most interesting findings was which feelings changed the least for the group over five years. These were guilt and anger. Guilt had been reported initially by 39 percent of mothers, and five years later was still reported by 34 percent of mothers; anger was reported initially by 40 percent of mothers and five years later by 34 percent of mothers. There was also little overall change reported for shame and emptiness. Thus bitterness for the group drops sharply over the years; sadness, worry, and nervousness decline; relief and thankfulness rise; but guilt, anger, and shame tend to persist.

Feelings have been reported for the overall sample of 160 mothers, but within the group there were shifts for individual mothers, some of whom abandoned and some of whom took on different feelings over the five-year period. To determine the extent to which the same mothers expressed the same feelings at time I and time III, the intercorrelations of feelings were determined. Although they were not high, six correlations were worth noting, three significant at $P \leqq .001$, and three significant at $P \leqq .05$. The first three are guilty $(r = .32)$, thankful $(r = .31)$, and relieved $(r = .30)$. These are the feelings that persist most strongly for the same women. The other stable feelings are angry $(r = .17)$, empty $(r = .16)$, and worried $(r = .16)$.

The data were analyzed to see if the expressions of feelings were related to the key study variables. Two factors, socioeconomic status of the mother and placement status of the child (in or out of care), were not significantly related to any of the feelings in the study in any particular way. Two other factors, religion of mother and sex of child, were related to one particular feeling. Catholic mothers were more likely to be sad and mothers of boys were more likely to be thankful with regard to the placement.

In three instances feelings were related to two variables each. Mothers with children placed for socially acceptable reasons were significantly more thankful; mothers with children placed for socially disapproved reasons were significantly more angry.[2] Type of placement was relevant in that mothers with children in residential treatment centers were significantly more thankful and more guilty than other mothers. There were no substantial differences in feelings reported by mothers with children in institutions other than treatment centers as against those in foster home care.

Two study variables, ethnicity and necessity of placement, showed significant differences in relation to four of the expressed feelings. Puerto Rican mothers expressed significantly higher levels of sadness, nervousness, and thankfulness, and significantly lower levels of guilt, than did white or Black mothers. Those mothers who felt that it had been absolutely necessary to place their children expressed less bitterness than others, whereas those who saw no necessity for placement expressed significantly less relief or thankfulness, and significantly more anger.

[2] For reasons included in each category, see chapter 1, "Basic Study Concepts."

Feeling Referents

Each time a mother reported experiencing one of the ten feelings on the checklist, she was asked, "about what or about whom?" From the spontaneous responses to that question seven categories were developed. Referents, defined as to what or to whom the feeling was referred, were as follows: self; self-child or separation; child; other interpersonal; agency-child or placement; agency itself; generalized other or society. At the time of the first interview, for all feelings combined, the referent most frequently reported was self, the second was the placement, the third was the separation, the fourth was other interpersonal, and the fifth was the child. Five years later referents were examined, again for all feelings expressed. At that time the most frequently noted referent was the child, the second was the separation, the third was self, the fourth was the placement, and the fifth was the agency. Interpersonal referents dropped to sixth place. The shift is of interest. At the time of placement, feelings were primarily referred to self and to the placement. Five years later the leading two referents were the child and the separation. Although the differences were not substantial, the passage of time meant that mothers were less concerned with self and with other adults, and were more likely to focus on the child.

Different feelings tended to call forth different referents, but an examination of each separate feelings-referents set showed that there was a shift in combinations over the five-year placement period. Separation remained the key referent for sadness both at placement and five years later, and the placement remained the main referent for thankfulness. The referent for anger, however, changed. At placement about 50 percent of the anger expressed was interpersonal, and 25 percent was directed against agencies. Five years later 40 percent of angry feelings were toward agencies, and only 25 percent against other persons. Interpersonal referents for bitterness also dropped from 60 percent at placement to 22 percent five years later, with an accompanying rise in agency referents for bitterness. Self-referents for guilt and shame dropped over the years, and guilt and shame were increasingly referred to the separation of mother and child. References to the placement for relief, nervousness, and worry tended to fall, and references to the child tended to rise.

Characteristics of individual mothers whose feelings changed over time were examined. The changes reported here all refer to statistically significant movement, which could not have been due to chance alone. Of those mothers who were not initially angry but became angry over the five-year period, significantly more were mothers whose children were placed for socially disapproved reasons. Neglect and abuse cases and cases of severe family dysfunction were prominent among those showing rise in anger. Thus the follow-up data reinforced the earlier findings—not only are more of the mothers in these categories angry to begin with, but more of them who were not initially angry become so over time.

A similar reinforcement was seen with regard to necessity of placement. The increase in feelings of relief and thankfulness was significantly higher for those mothers who saw placement as absolutely necessary, and the increase in anger was significantly higher for those who saw placement as not at all necessary. Increase in anger was higher for mothers with negative feelings about placement; increase in thankfulness was higher for mothers with positive feelings. Furthermore, increase in anger was high where mothers reported low caseworker interest in their problems, whereas for those mothers who reported high caseworker interest, relief increased and shame decreased.

To study how feelings grouped themselves, and whether these groupings persisted over time, a factor analysis was completed on all feelings expressed by mothers at placement and about placement five years later. The statistical technique involves intercorrelations, so that the relationships among the variables can be determined. Those sets of variables that "go together" form identifiable factors.

Both at the initial interview and five years later, there were four factors that could be identified, with comparable feeling components. The first of these can be labeled an "anxiety" factor, with high factor loadings on the feelings of sadness, nervousness, and worry expressed at both times. The second factor is "benign gratitude," and includes low anger and high relief and thankfulness. The third factor is strongest on guilt but also includes shame. The fourth factor is high on anger, and also includes bitterness. These are the four main groupings of feelings seen both at placement and five years later.

A final analytic approach to these data was through the technique of cluster analysis. The study of feelings has shown that each individual parent has a combination of feelings, sometimes conflicting, sometimes reinforcing, but always complex rather than unidimensional. The research question was whether individual reaction patterns could be identified and grouped into a typology of parental feeling syndromes. Furthermore, if such syndromes could be identified, were they related to other variables and characteristics of the population? If such links could be established, they would be revealing of the relationships of feeling patterns to client characteristics.

Cluster analysis organizes a set of responses into groups based on internal similarities, with no prior hypothesis. This technique was used to determine groups of mothers, based on their feeling patterns. It differs from the previously used factor analysis technique in that "factors" refer to combinations of feelings and not clusters of mothers.

At time I, directly after placement, there were three distinct clusters, designated as group A, with 71 members, group B, with 60 members, and group C, with 21 members.[3]

Mothers in group A were significantly higher than others on 7 of the 10 feelings—sad, angry, nervous, bitter, and worried—and lower on relieved and thankful. For example, only 16 percent of mothers in group A were thankful, and 70 percent were angry.

Group B presented a very different constellation of feelings; these mothers were significantly high on sad, relieved, and thankful,

[3] A full presentation of cluster data can be found in Jenkins and Norman, *Filial Deprivation*, pp. 117–37. In addition there were two small clusters, with four members each, which will be considered idiosyncratic and disregarded for purposes of this analysis.

and low on angry, nervous, ashamed, empty, bitter, worried, and guilty. Among these mothers 80 percent were thankful, and not one expressed shame.

Group C mothers were distinguished by being high on relieved, ashamed, empty, thankful, and guilty. In particular, every mother in this group said she felt guilty.

The overlapping of feelings makes it hard to draw sharp lines, since certain feelings are common to many mothers. The anxiety factor is pervasive, but it drops out of the cluster analysis because worry and sadness are such common feelings they become a generalized component across several clusters. Significant clusters can only be identified through the primary feelings that are unique to each: group A mothers are angry and bitter; group B mothers are relieved and thankful; and group C mothers are guilty.

The primary clusters of mothers at placement were therefore the angry group, the thankful group, and the guilty group. In addition to feelings, these groups also differed significantly on several key study variables, although some mothers from each cluster could be found in all categories. For cluster A, for example—the angry group—53 percent had socially unacceptable reasons for placement, which was the case for only 17 percent of group B and 24 percent of group C. Other distinguishing characteristics of cluster A were that they were 90 percent Black and Puerto Rican; that they were relatively highest in the placement category of neglect and abuse; that 44 percent of these mothers believed placement was absolutely unnecessary—as compared to 2 and 5 percent, respectively, for the other groups; that over half of these mothers had the lowest socioeconomic scores in the sample; and that they scored highest of the groups on alienation, with a mean anomie score of 3.1.

For cluster B, the mothers who were relieved and thankful, 83 percent of the children were placed for socially acceptable reasons. The largest placement category was child behavior, followed by physical illness of the mother, and the largest ethnic group was white. Furthermore, 53 percent of these mothers saw placement as absolutely necessary and 32 percent as somewhat necessary; 45 percent of them were in the highest socioeconomic group, and their mean anomie score was 2.6—a low level of alienation for the study sample.

Finally, for cluster C, mothers who felt guilt, the most distinguishing characteristic was the relatively high percentage of children placed because of mental illness of the mother. There was not one mother in this group whose child was placed because of her physical illness. These mothers fell in the middle of the socioeconomic scale and they were also moderate in alienation. They saw the necessity of placement, but not quite so strongly as mothers in group B. There were significantly more Catholic mothers in this group than in the other two. These findings support the hypothesis that groups of mothers with identifiable feeling syndromes will also have identifiable social and demographic characteristics.

By the time of the third field interview, there had been some changes in the cluster patterns, to be anticipated since some feelings rose and some declined. There was a reduction of sharp distinctions, and the four clusters that were thrown up from the analysis were of quite different sizes. A large cluster, which can be labeled cluster D, contained 103 members. This was distinguished from all others primarily by the absence of anger, shame, bitterness, or guilt. Anxiety factors were present, but these were held in common with other clusters. In addition, there were three small clusters, labeled E, F, and G, with 28, 11, and 15 members. One was primarily angry, one primarily guilty, and the third expressed both anger and guilt.

In comparison with the cluster analysis of the same mothers five years earlier, this grouping is much less discriminatory. It is hypothesized that, for the large majority of mothers, feelings were less intense; in a sense, they regressed to the mean. For most mothers time had obliterated some of the sharp differences seen at placement, although small groups persisted in feeling anger and guilt. If it is to be useful in working with families, the feelings analysis should be utilized directly after placement, since that is when groups can best be identified.

Mothers' Estimates
of Childrens' Feelings

At the time of the last field interview, when 74 percent of the children had been discharged, mothers were asked how they thought their children had felt about placement. In general, mothers reported fewer feeling responses for children than they had for themselves. The rank ordering of feelings, however, was close to that of the mothers $(r = .80)$.[4]

Sadness was reported by mothers as being felt by 49 percent of children; worry was next common, reported for 41 percent. Feelings expressed least frequently were shame and guilt, with mothers reporting these as felt by only 12 and 7 percent of children, respectively. These two feelings may not have been perceived as "childlike" by the mother respondents.

In all cases except two, feelings mothers reported for their children were significantly different from those expressed for themselves. There was closeness in feelings reported with regard to anger and bitterness. Five years after placement 34 percent of mothers said they were angry, and 27 percent said their children were angry. There were 24 percent who said they were bitter, and 21 percent said their children were bitter. Whether the responses were a valid report of the child's true feelings or a projection on the part of the mother, they tell something about the nature of these particular feelings as compared with other feelings that were held by mothers but not, according to them, by their children.

Feelings at Discharge

In the field interview most closely following in time the return home of the child from care, mothers were asked about their feelings on

[4] See table 3.

discharge. Responses were secured from 110 women, and the percentages reporting experiencing various feelings are noted in table 3.

The shift in reported reactions from placement to discharge is dramatic. Thankfulness was the main feeling at discharge, being reported by 83 percent of mothers whose children returned home. The other strong feeling was relief, expressed by 68 percent of mothers. The two other feelings worth noting, experienced by 33 and 28 percent of mothers, respectively, were nervousness and worry. Other feelings dropped to negligible levels.

The responses on discharge by individual mothers were analyzed to see if they tended to be primarily related to the situation or were typical of the particular respondent. The two strongest responses on discharge, thankfulness and relief, had only been experienced on placement by about half of those mothers who reported these feelings on discharge, 56 percent for thankfulness and 44 percent for relief. The other feelings reported on discharge, nervousness and worry, had also been felt on entry to placement by 80 percent and 78 percent, respectively, of the mothers who reported them later. The interpretation which is suggested is that thankfulness and relief were more situation-related, specifically aroused by the discharge. Nervousness and worry, however, were felt on placement by the great majority who felt them on discharge. These feelings reflect those mothers' own emotional reactions to crisis and change, whether for the worse or the better.

Over half of all mothers, when asked what they worried about while children were in care, said they were concerned about the separation and worried about what would happen to their relationship with their children. The feelings of relief and thankfulness expressed on discharge did not mean that all the problems were solved.

Mothers were articulate in expressing concerns about how the placement affected the child-parent relationship. One said that after discharge home, "The children had changed; I felt treated like a stranger. It took a long time for them to trust me." Another mother said, "We lost the battle of trying to make it together. I felt depressed." One mother said, "The three years he was away I felt I didn't have a son—I didn't see his daily growth and share in his growing. I really don't know him and I didn't have him." Still another mother said, "Things are worse for me now. The children are older and they don't respect me." Another mother said, "I was loaded with guilt feelings. I was never able to conquer the feeling that in some ways placement was unnecessary."

One mother said, "I am faced with the problem that my child does not want to visit us now. I suffered in giving birth to my child and there is nothing good about placement because I feel I am still alive but the placement makes the children feel that I am dead."

These are illustrations of the filial deprivation effects of the placement experience. What comes through from the women quoted are expressions of unworthiness, of ineffectiveness and impotence in meeting filial expectations. It is impossible to estimate how much of the distance these mothers feel from their children is due to the child's growing older and more independent, and how much to the separation. The responses were not all in one direction—for some mothers the separation, although keenly felt, was viewed as necessary and helpful. For others, it further weakened the already shaky family foundations.

Four

Mothers
Evaluate
Placement

Five years after their children entered foster care approximately half of the 186 mothers who responded to the final field interview [1] expressed positive, satisfied feelings about the placement experience; about one-fourth were negative and disapproving, and the remaining one-fourth were ambivalent, neutral, or noncommittal. These proportions held for both mothers whose children were discharged and those whose children remained in care, with no significant difference between the groups on their placement evaluation.

The positive reactions to foster care were usually expressed by mothers in terms of the circumstances under which placement occurred. Most mothers did not say, "Placement is a good thing," but rather that, considering the situation in which they found themselves, it was an acceptable and even a satisfying child-care arrangement. One

[1] The figure 186 represents all mother respondents to the last field interview, of whom 160 had also been seen at the initial survey. Where change data are analyzed, the *N* of 160 is used; where the placement evaluation represents reactions at one time only, the additional 26 mothers who could not be seen initially are included.

mother, for example, said, "It was good for them since I could not take care of them because I was ill." Another said, "It was the best thing that could have happened to me; it gave me a chance to get back on my feet, a chance to grow up and really be a mother to my children." A third mother said, "I feel good about foster care. It helped me when I couldn't help myself." Some mothers were able to be very open in response to the interviewer. One said, "I didn't like to talk about it, but now I can be frank. Placement was the best thing. If my daughter had stayed with me I would have killed her. I used to beat her and scream at her until the neighbors reported me. Once she made me so angry that I placed her hands in hot water. I guess I hated her because I hated her father and I was glad she was placed. Now the caseworker is trying to help her come back to me. It will take a long while but I hope I will get her back. It will not be easy. I still get annoyed but not as much. . . ."

The negative responses from one-fourth of the mothers were based primarily on objections to agency control over the child, to the child's experiences in care, and to the separation. Here are examples of each of these reactions, in the words of the clients. One mother said, "People just try to get the children so they can get the money. Institutions and foster parents want the money." Another mother said, "It's true that when he was placed, he gave me a lot of trouble, but at the institution where he is the boys beat him and he comes home to visit in a terrible condition."

Examples of ambivalent or neutral responses from mothers were, "Sometimes I feel good about it, sometimes bad"; "They don't give as much love, but they take good care"; and "I don't feel good about it, but it has to be that way."

Strong positive and negative feelings on the part of mothers emerged from the interviews, and these cases were analyzed to see what variables were characteristic of families in each group. One of the main factors related to reactions to foster care was the reason for placement. Among the various placement reasons, those that were related to a positive feeling about foster care were situations in which children had entered care because of the mother's mental illness, her physical illness, the child's emotional behavior, or the mother's unwillingness to assume care of an infant, primarily those born out of wedlock. These have already been identified as the "socially acceptable" reasons. Negative responses to the placement experience came more frequently from mothers who had been unwilling to continue care of an older child, from families in which there was neglect or abuse, abandonment of children, or severe family dysfunction. These have been called the "socially disapproved" reasons. When grouped into these two main categories, socially approved and socially unacceptable, and tested for their positive, negative, and ambivalent reactions of mothers to placement, significant differences emerge $(\chi^2 = 18.8; P \leqq .001)$.

Satisfaction with placement was also related to the three key demographic variables of ethnicity, religion, and socioeconomic status. For example, more positive attitudes than average were expressed by white mothers and Jewish mothers, more negative attitudes by Puerto Rican mothers and Catholic mothers. It was found that positive attitudes were directly related to the families with the highest socioeconomic circumstances, and negative attitudes were directly related to the lowest socioeconomic scores.

The socioeconomic differences, shown in table 4, are highly significant $(P \leqq .001)$. Positive attitudes toward foster care were expressed by 60 percent of the high group, 44 percent of the middle, and 36 percent of the low socioeconomic group. Negative attitudes were expressed by only 10 percent of the high, 27 percent of the middle, and 31 percent of the low group. This finding warrants investigation. It is not enough to assume that higher income groups are generally more satisfied and less critical consumers. The question to investigate is whether in fact they were getting the same services or whether they were being delivered a superior product to that received by the lowest socioeconomic group.

Table 4. Reactions to Care by Socioeconomic Status of Mother: Percentage Distribution (N = 186)

	Socioeconomic Level		
Reactions	*High*	*Middle*	*Low*
Total	*100*	*100*	*100*
Positive	60	44	36
Negative	10	27	31
Neutral, Ambivalent	30	29	33

Both at entry to care and five years later, mothers were asked how necessary they felt placement to be. In general, the more necessary the mothers felt placement to be, the more they tended to have positive feelings about the foster-care experience. Furthermore, only 12 percent of mothers who said at entry that placement was "not at all necessary" had positive feelings about foster care; 46 percent had negative feelings.

Positive feelings about placement tend to be relatively higher from mothers of older children in the sample, who were six years or more at the time of placement; and negative feelings were higher for children who were from six months to under six years at placement. There was a special reaction, however, from mothers of babies placed from birth to under six months. These infants were primarily newborn and born out of wedlock, and their mothers had significantly fewer negative feelings about foster care.

With regard to sex of the child there was a significant difference in the expression of positive and negative feelings ($P \leq .05$): 53 percent of mothers with only boys in placement expressed positive responses, as compared with 40 percent of mothers with only girls in placement. Moreover, 22 percent of mothers with only boys in care expressed negative reactions, whereas these were expressed by 48 percent of mothers with only girls in care. Others were ambivalent or neutral. (For this analysis mothers with two children, one of each sex, were excluded from the total.)

Beyond the general positive and negative reactions to foster care, the interviewers probed for specific reasons why mothers reacted as they did, and for illustrations of how placement affected their children and themselves. Of those mothers who said they had generally positive reactions to placement, one-third specifically referred to the good care the children were getting as the main positive factor. The comments about good care were made by significantly more mothers whose children were in placement because of the mothers' mental or physical illness, or their own unwillingness to assume child care. Good care was particularly stressed by mothers with children from six months to under two years.

Nineteen percent of mothers thought their children were functioning better, and this was expressed by a significantly higher proportion of mothers whose children had been discharged than by those whose children were still in care. These reactions about functioning were made in particular by white mothers and referred to significantly more of the older children who had been placed because of their own emotional problems.

Twelve percent of mothers, more of whose children were in care than discharged, reported that the children were receiving a good education while in placement. This was particularly noted by mothers of older children. Proportionately, educational advantages were reported by twice as many of the Puerto Rican mothers, or 24 percent. An "improved environment" was also noted as a placement advantage, and this tended to be reported by Black Protestant mothers. Finally, a number of mothers mentioned that there were substantial material advantages for children while in foster care.

Mothers were very specific when they reported ways in which care benefited children. With regard to material advantages, for example, one mother said, "They made a 'mensch' out of him. Because they taught him how to clean his room, do work with self-reliance. In June he will graduate from vocational school and be able to get a job." Another mother said that her child got things in foster care he had never had at home—a better school, Big Brothers, and music lessons. Another said, "He has opportunities which I could not give him—sports, amusement parks and museums.'' There were several cases in which mothers stressed the value to the child of being away from a bad environment. One said, ''It was good for him because he was hanging around with the wrong crowd and not going to school.''

There were also a number of mothers who said that foster care was bad for their child, but their responses to the interviewers' probes were not as specific as those of mothers with positive reactions. The negative responses were in three major areas: (1) that foster care was bad for the child because the relationship with the mother suffered; (2) that the child suffered emotionally; and (3) that he suffered in a developmental sense.

Discharge status was related to the kinds of negative effects reported by mothers. A relatively higher proportion of mothers whose children were still in care said that their relationship with their child was suffering. This response was given by a proportionately higher percentage of Puerto Rican mothers, and as far as they were concerned this was the most negative aspect of foster care. The response that the child was suffering emotionally was given more frequently by the lowest socioeconomic group, whereas the response that the child was suffering developmentally was given by mothers of the highest socioeconomic group. With regard to age, concern about the emotional suffering of the child was expressed to a greater extent by mothers of children in the age category from two years to under six.

A number of the more explicit negative comments on foster care were made by those mothers whose children had been discharged, and who were coping with their reintegration into the family. One mother, for example, said, ''I had to go through a readjustment period with the children. They had a feeling of not being wanted by me.'' Another said, ''It was difficult for him to adjust to being home with me; he felt strange being away from his other place.'' A third mother said, ''They gave her too much freedom there so when she came home she was too wild. They bought her anything she wanted and she became spoiled.''

Mothers with positive responses to foster care were specifically asked how placement was good for them. Some responses were self-referred, but others expressed their feelings about their children. Thirty-five percent of the positive mothers said that placement was good for them because it freed them from worry about the children. This response was particularly high from mothers who had been physically ill, or whose children were emotionally disturbed. The next largest group, 28 percent, said placement helped them cope with their own emotional problems. These were primarily mothers of infants, who had been unwilling to assume their care. Another 17 percent said there was an indirect benefit in that what was good for their children was good for themselves. This response was given primarily by mothers whose children had been placed because of neglect or abuse.

About one-third of the mothers reported that the best thing about placement was that it relieved them of worry about their children, whereas another one-third reported that the worst thing about placement was that it caused them to worry. These data show that there are no simple responses, and reactions reflect the individual respondent, the child, and the situation both before and after placement.

Some of the mothers' individual comments about why placement was good for them were revealing. One mother said, "I was wrong and it made me a better mother. It taught me a lesson." Another said, "I didn't have that responsibility. She was there and I was free; I didn't have to hit her and hurt her anymore."

There was evidence that other family members, in addition to mothers, were responding to the child being in foster care. One-third of the families reported that siblings at home had been affected by children's placements; next in importance were maternal grandparents; and third, the other parent. These reactions were significantly different according to ethnic groups. Black mothers emphasized the effect on the siblings, white mothers mostly said it was the other parent, and Puerto Rican mothers stressed the effect on the maternal grandparent.

Responses to Workers

In addition to reporting the impact of placement on themselves and on their children, mothers were asked to evaluate some of the specific components of the foster care experience. Important among these was their response to caseworker activity. Four areas were explored: mothers were asked to report the extent to which the agency caseworker

1. "was interested in you as a person and wanted to help";
2. "understood you and what you were going through";
3. "helped you meet your personal and family needs"; and
4. "informed you as to how your child was getting along. . . ."

Responses were noted on a three-point scale in which 1 indicated "not at all"; 2, "somewhat"; and 3, "very much." Scores on each item could therefore range from 1 to 3. The mean score for caseworker interest was 2.3; for caseworker understanding, 2.2; for caseworker helpfulness, 1.9; and for caseworker communication, 2.3. Although not large, the differences show that, in general, mothers rated caseworkers' interest, understanding, and communication higher than they rated their helpfulness.

Reason for placement was significantly related to the way in which mothers perceived caseworkers. For example, there were significantly lower scores in all categories for those mothers whose children were placed for what have been called the socially unacceptable reasons for placement, including neglect and abuse, abandonment, and family dysfunction. Significantly higher scores in all areas were noted for mothers whose children were placed because of the socially approved reasons, i.e., physical or mental illness, inability to assume care, and child behavior. Furthermore, there was a continuum for scores in direct relationship to the socioeconomic circumstances of the family. The higher the socioeconomic group, the more likely was the mother, regardless of reason for placement or any other characteristic, to perceive the caseworker as interested, helpful, understanding, and communicative.

Another significant distinction can be made between responses of mothers with children in care and those of mothers whose children had been discharged. Mothers whose children had been discharged scored workers as more helpful, interested, understanding, and communicative than did mothers with children still in care. It should be noted there was no relationship seen between ethnic group and mothers' perceptions of workers in any of the four areas.

These data do not reflect an objective view of actual worker performance, but rather how workers were perceived by the mothers. Reactions to workers generally follow the overall maternal reactions to placement, a finding for the practice field to consider. Is it that the potential for working with mothers whose children have entered care for socially unacceptable reasons is so much less because of their own pathology? Is it that the agencies which serve these mothers offer less in relation to their greater needs? Or is it that there may be an implied rejection of them by caseworkers? Whatever the explanation, client perceptions of their workers call for attention, since the relationship is a transaction in which the input of all parties bears examination.

Visiting Patterns and Problems

Of all the aspects of foster care, one of the most controversial and generally unsatisfying is the visiting of children by their biological parents. There are many different factors that enter into visiting patterns, not all of which are easy to evaluate. Children may enter care because of physical or mental illness with accompanying institutionalization of parents, so that with the best will in the world, mothers simply are not able to visit. On the other hand, mothers may want to visit, but sporadically and in a way that may be disturbing to both child and foster parents. Some agencies encourage and facilitate visiting, by making arrangements and providing transportation; others react to foster parent pressures to limit visiting as being disruptive to the placement. Many child care institutions are some distance from the parental home. Parents on welfare cannot afford expensive carfare, non-English-speaking parents may not easily travel, or working parents may not be able to get time off. All parties give lip service to "keeping families together," but when disruption has already occurred, where and how best to strengthen tenuous ties is a complicated problem. One of the most knotty issues is the prediction of relationships over time. Will the difficult task of maintaining regular visiting patterns, even if somewhat disruptive to the placement adjustment and expensive and exhausting for agency and caretaker, pay off in the long run by facilitating discharge and easing readjustment in the home of the biological parent? No one answer will meet all cases, but the underlying philosophy of visiting should be clear to all parties.

Data on visiting comes from mothers' own reports, and may therefore be overstated. There is, however, substantial range in responses, and patterns do relate in a meaningful way to other study variables. In the field surveys mothers were asked how often they had visited children over the preceding six months or, if children had been discharged, during the last six months in care. These data were more reliable than information on visiting directly after placement, since they reflected a more stable pattern, with likelihood of access by more parents.

Over a six-month period when care had been stabilized, 48 percent of mothers reported that they visited their placed children at least once every two weeks, 16 percent visited once a month, 19 percent less than once a month, and 13 percent not at all. Visiting for 4 percent was not ascertainable. Frequency of visiting was related to the type of placement, with the least visiting occurring when children were in foster homes. Those children were visited at least once a month by only 51 percent of mothers, as compared to minimal monthly visits by 73 percent of mothers with children in institutions and 78 percent of those with children in residential treatment centers. Children in foster homes tended to be the youngest in the sample. White and Puerto Rican mothers (73 percent and 70 percent, respectively) visited at least once a month, with only 55 percent of Black mothers visiting at that frequency. In general, the higher the socioeconomic status of the family, the more frequent were the visits.

After placement had stabilized, those children placed because of the mother's physical illness were visited most frequently: 63 percent were visited at least once every two weeks and another 17 percent were visited about once a month. Although the illness prevented child care, visiting was apparently possible for most mothers. The disturbed children were visited next most frequently, with 58 percent of their mothers visiting every two weeks and 13 percent visiting once a month. In cases of neglect and abuse, there was the least amount of visiting, with fewer than 45 percent of mothers visiting once a month and about 20 percent not visiting at all.

Only one-fourth of all mothers said that they had no problems visiting their children; the rest reported one or more complaints or difficulties. Of those with problems, about half of the mothers said their own illness prevented them from visiting as much as they would have liked. Of the other major problems mentioned, over one-third of all mothers mentioned the distance from the child and the lack of travel money as creating problems. The foster care establishment was blamed for setting inconvenient visiting times by about 20 percent of mothers, and the same percentage accused agencies of trying to keep the mothers away. Eleven percent of the mothers blamed the foster parents themselves for making visiting difficult. Finally, one-third of the mothers felt that visiting was upsetting emotionally for themselves, and one-fourth said that it was disturbing for the child.

The reason for placement appears to be related to problems in visiting. "No problem" in visiting was reported most frequently by those mothers whose children were placed for "child behavior." As might be expected, prolonged illness was reported most frequently by those mothers whose children were placed because of the mother's physical or emotional illness. The number of problems reported also appears to be related to the reason for placement, with mothers whose children were placed for "family dysfunction" reporting the largest number of problems (averaging over 3 per case). Those cases in which the reason for placement was "socially disapproved" averaged more problems in visiting than those in which the reason was "socially acceptable."

The difficulties mentioned by mothers are reflected in the frequency of visits. Those mothers who reported no problems visited most frequently. Least visiting was done by the 17 women who said that they "did not know how to arrange visits" (one-third of these women did not visit at all). Also doing less visiting than most were those who reported that the agency did not allow visiting (one-fifth did not visit at all). Illness, lack of money, and inconvenient visiting times were frequently listed as problems by those mothers who visited less than once a month. On the other hand, those mothers who said that visiting tended to upset them or the children were among the most frequent visitors.

About half of the mothers felt that the agencies could have made visiting easier, primarily by making the visiting times more convenient, and also by having children placed closer to home. Differences in attitudes about whether agencies could facilitate visiting were significantly related to type of placement. Of those mothers with children in residential treatment centers, 78 percent felt that there was no way the agency could make visiting easier, whereas 70 percent of mothers with children in foster homes felt that the agency could do something to help, in particular by making visiting times more convenient and by placing children closer to home. Mothers with children in other children's institutions were divided; about half felt that there were ways the agency could facilitate visiting. Although 27 percent of all mothers included lack of money for carfare as a problem in visiting, only 4 percent of them mentioned it as the main way in which the agency could have helped. So although money is a problem, it is apparently not one that mothers perceive should be resolved by the placement agency. Instead, mothers on public assistance tend to turn to that source for support.[2]

Ninety-four percent of the mothers visited their children at one time or another during placement. A continuum of frequency of visits has been described, but there are no absolute standards. How much visiting do mothers perceive to be "enough"? Over half of the mothers (58 percent) felt that they had not visited enough, including those who visited at least once every two weeks, whereas the rest of the mothers felt that they had visited enough. Of the mothers who felt they did not visit enough, the main problem for those who visited less frequently was illness; the main problem for those who visited more frequently was agency policy.

Mothers perceived their children to be less satisfied than they were with the frequency of visiting, with 73 percent of mothers judging that their children wanted more visiting. Perception of satisfaction of children was not related to actual frequency of visiting, with satisfied children being visited about as often as children reported as unsatisfied.

General Attitudes to Agencies: Changes Over Time

In spite of the variety of experiences of mothers while children were in care, their general attitudes toward foster agencies did not change to any significant degree over the five-year period. At the time of placement respondents were asked whether they saw agencies as facilitators of child care, as usurpers of parental rights, or as surrogates for parents. The same questions were repeated five years later, and the major finding was the persistence of group attitudes, with no signifi-

---

[2] The problem of securing carfare to visit children in foster homes was raised by welfare clients in a special survey conducted by the Community Council of Greater New York. See *Problems With Income Maintenance and Services at the Department of Social Service* (New York: Community Council of Greater New York, Inc., May 1973).

cant differences whatsoever between attitudes of all mothers at entry and five years later. This is not to say that some individuals did not change their responses. Approximately half of all mothers gave exactly the same answers, but the changes that did occur for the other half tended to balance out, so that, overall, the group scores were identical at both field surveys.

Further analysis by some of the key variables utilized in the study, such as ethnic group, religion, and socioeconomic status, also did not show any significant changes in attitudes toward agencies over time. In terms of reason for placement, the only change was among mentally ill mothers, who saw agencies as significantly less facilitating after five years than at the time of placement.

One variable that was of particular interest in relation to attitudes to agencies was whether children were in or out of care at the time of the final interview. Mothers with children still in care tended to find agencies as fulfilling more of a usurper role than those whose children had been discharged. Perception of the agency as a surrogate was also stronger by mothers whose children were still in care after five years. Thus the factor that does affect maternal attitudes is the persistence of the agency responsibility for the child, rather than the experience of the family with the agency while the child is in care.

Intergroup differences in attitudes to agencies also persisted over time. Highest usurper scores both at entry and five years later were held by families whose children were placed because of abandonment, neglect or abuse, and family dysfunction. Highest usurper scores were also related at all times in the study to those families with the lowest socioeconomic status. On the surrogate component, Puerto Rican families had been significantly different from both white and Black families at entry in tending to regard the agency as a surrogate for child care. An analysis of data for the same mothers from the final interview showed the Puerto Rican mothers continuing to see agencies in the surrogate role to a significantly greater extent than either Black or white mothers.

Not only did attitudes toward agencies persist over the five-year study period; the general social attitudes of families also remained almost constant. The main measurement used was the Srole anomie scale, a widely accepted measure of alienation.[3] The initial score for mothers indicated high general alienation, and this did not change over the five years. The 160 mothers achieved a mean score of 2.86 on the alienation scale in 1966, and their score in 1971 was 2.94.

An examination of alienation scores by all the critical study variables revealed only one subgroup in which significant change occurred. This is the group of mothers whose children entered placement because of their unwillingness to assume care at the time of birth. They were primarily young unmarried mothers who did not wish to surrender children for adoption. Shortly after the birth of the children, in the initial survey, this group tended to score lower in alienation than did other mothers in the study with placed children. Five years later, however, there was a significant rise in the alienation scores of the young unmarried mothers, and they were no longer significantly different from any other group in the study with regard level of anomie.

Since there were no changes in alienation scores in relation to any other study variables, including reason for placement, ethnic group, socioeconomic status, or religion, the change noted for the young unmarried group is of particular interest. These were the least experienced mothers, and initially were more hopeful, more ready to see a future for themselves and to trust other people than were the other mothers in the study. In the five years after the placement, they

---

[3] The items used from the Srole scale are as follows:

1. These days a person doesn't really know who he can count o
2. In spite of what people say, the lot of the average man is getting worse, not better.
3. Most public officials are not really interested in the problems of the average man.
4. Nowadays, a person has to live pretty much for today and let tomorrow take care of itself.
5. It's hardly fair to bring children into the world the way things look for the future.

For a further discussion of the Srole Scale, see Shirley Jenkins and Elaine Norman, *Filial Deprivation and Foster Care* (New York: Columbia University Press, 1972), pp. 144–45.

had grown in experience, and their alienation from others and from society had risen.

Evaluation Summary

In summary, how do mothers evaluate foster care? The findings show that about half are satisfied, one-quarter negative, and one-quarter neutral, ambivalent, or noncommittal. Is this typical of client response to service delivery? Only when client evaluations of services become a routine part of evaluation studies will there be enough data to develop an empirical yardstick against which to measure whether a 50-percent satisfaction rate is good, bad, or typical.

With regard to specific responses made by mothers on both negative and positive aspects of care, one finding is that mothers frequently refer to the experiences of the child as well as to factors associated with their separation from the child. In the analysis of maternal responses to placement at the time of the initial interview, it was noted that mothers were very self-centered and self-involved. The follow-up data appears to reflect a shift in primary maternal concerns from self to the child and to the separation. This may mean that the five years since placement have given mothers a chance to meet some of their own needs or solve some of their own problems, and thus freed them to pay appropriate attention to their children and their maternal roles.

A third major finding from the evaluation data is that positive reactions to placement were strongest in families in the highest socioeconomic status. This association was also seen in mothers' reactions to workers, and in their evaluations of workers' helpfulness, interest, understanding, and communication with them. A further variable associated with positive evaluation of placement was whether the reason for placement fell in the "socially approved" or in the "socially unacceptable" category. Thus where children were placed because of the mother's physical or mental illness, the child's emotional problems, or the young unmarried mother's unwillingness or inability to assume care of her infant, maternal evaluations of placement and of workers are significantly more positive than where children are placed because of abandonment, neglect or abuse, family dysfunction, or unwillingness or inability to continue care. The interpretation of this finding is not obvious, and the area needs further research. There may be different levels or kinds of pathology in the two groups, with the latter being more alienated and antisocial, which in turn affects their attitudes to any institutional effort. Worker attitudes may also vary, and the mothers in the more alienated group may also be on the receiving end of negative and punitive worker-agency reactions. Finally, it may be that the foster care system itself tends to differentiate in placement, and that clients in the two different groups were in fact receiving a different level of services, that their children were placed in different kinds of agencies, and that the responses of mothers were valid reactions to the nature and quality of services offered.

As a final question on placement evaluation, mothers were asked whether they would suggest foster care to other families facing the same problems; 57 percent of mothers said no, and 43 percent said yes. Responses were not significantly related to ethnic group, socioeconomic status, or placement status. A significant difference did, however, emerge with regard to reason for placement. Those mothers whose children had been placed for either of the two following reasons, physical illness of the mother or her unwillingness to assume care (primarily of out-of-wedlock newborn infants), strongly recommended placement for mothers with similar problems. This was the case for 74 percent of the physically ill mothers, and 88 percent of those who did not assume care of infants. In all other placement categories the majority of mothers were against recommending placement. Thus the mothers' evaluation of their own placement experience was more favorable than their stance in recommending the service for others.

Interviewers probed for the reasons behind this response, and the seeming contradiction was clarified. Mothers saw foster care as a last resort to be undertaken only when there was no possible alternative. They did not see it as a solution to their problems, and felt that no benefits had accrued from placement. Mothers seemed to be saying they accepted doing what they had to do, but they hesitated to recommend it because, even though they couldn't name it, "There must be a better way."

Five

Resources
and
Problem
Solving

A classic question for evaluation studies of agency services is, "Does the 'help' help?" Where there are clearly defined objectives, this question may be answered by measuring the extent to which outcome approaches goals. The evaluation of foster care intervention, however, typically occurs against a constantly shifting scene, since family situations do not remain the same but may either worsen or improve because of factors totally unrelated to the original reason for placement. Furthermore, findings on the usefulness of services depend not only on what is measured, but on who does the measuring.

Since the present study is concerned with the perceptions and experiences of biological mothers in relation to foster care, it is appropriate that the evaluation of what helped and what hurt in services be made by the clients themselves. The reactions to foster care services given by mothers will be supplemented by their reports on what other community resources were utilized, and the extent to which these resources were helpful. Differential use of services according to ethnic group, socioeconomic status, and reason for placement will also be discussed.

In addition to evaluation of services, client reactions on several other key issues, including ethnic and religious composition of agencies and proposals for primary prevention, are reported. Finally, mothers were asked what basic changes would have made a difference in their life situations and enabled them to avoid the problems of foster care. This question probed more deeply than inquiries on ameliorative or rehabilitative concerns, and sought to measure client perceptions of the etiology of their problems as well as proposals for primary prevention.

What Helped and What Hurt

Respondents were asked what in the last five years had affected the problems that had brought their children into placement, and whether these situations had been helped or aggravated. More than one factor could be mentioned by each mother. The responses fell into two major groupings, one dealing with people and the other with institutional or agency impact. The third factor was time itself.

In referring to people, mothers mentioned themselves, their children, and other persons. When asked who had the most important impact on their problems, 62 percent of the 186 mothers responded by saying "myself." Of this group, about 80 percent said they had helped themselves, 10 percent said they had made things worse for themselves, and the rest said what they did had both helped and hurt. Since "self" was named most frequently, the conclusion is that the majority of mothers saw their own efforts and their own capacities to cope as the most meaningful of all factors affecting their situations.

Mothers said they helped themselves in three main ways: in the areas of physical and mental health, jobs, and social adjustment. Several women, for example, said they kept doctor's appointments, stopped drinking (one by going to AA), took medicine, and followed prescribed regimens. Nine mothers said they secured help from psychiatrists or social workers. This last group primarily comprised mothers whose children were placed because of their own mental illness or the child's behavior.

Work as a problem-solving activity was most frequently reported to be the way women helped themselves. Ten mothers said they had obtained jobs, three were going to school for training, one other was in a WIN program. Finally, at least a dozen mothers stated they felt they had developed insight and improved their capacity to cope with their problems by their own efforts. One said she helped herself "by growing up and facing my responsibilities," and another said, "I talked to myself and found out my real problem—to realize things as they were." These are not unusual statements for any one mother to make. As a group, however, it is worth noting that one-third of the clients perceived help as coming from their own efforts and not as a result of a service offered. Even in terms of treatment, help was not reported as what the psychiatrist did, but what the mother did in seeking therapy. And school and job were not reported as services either, but as resulting from the clients' own reaching out.

Almost half of all mothers (44 percent) reported that the child was a factor in their changed situation over the last five years. Of these, two-thirds said the child helped things by improving in behavior or performance, and one-fourth said the child's behavior aggravated the situation. References to the child were made almost entirely by the child behavior cases. Typically, better behavior at home and in school was mentioned as leading to improvement, but worse behavior was also noted in some cases. Child behavior cases were probably the most amenable to evaluation on change, since the variables involved were most clearly defined.

The last personal factor reported was the effect of other individuals on their situations. Just over half of the mothers, 51 percent, said that other people had helped them with their problems; 33 percent said others had aggravated them. In terms of "relevant others," the husband was most frequently reported as both helping and hurting. This was followed by mention of the mother of the respondent. Relatives were very often condemned as taking children away from mothers, refusing to help, beating mothers, and pushing drugs. These data show that support of "others" was not always available for these families.

The reports on agency factors differentiated among types of agency contacts. Of the 51 percent of mothers who reported the placement agency as affecting their situation, just fewer than two-thirds said it helped them and one-third said it aggravated their problems. More favorable responses were accorded to the placement itself, mentioned by 48 percent of mothers. Of these, about three-fourths said the placement helped and one-fifth said it aggravated their problems. About the same reactions were reported to family agencies working with mothers.

When they mentioned the placement agency as affecting their problems, the main positive comments were in terms of the facilitative function—that is, that the agency assumed care when the mother could not carry on. Several parents said that agency sessions in which parents met with workers and were helped to understand their problems, or in which workers counseled parents, were extremely useful. On the negative side, agencies were criticized for keeping children from parents and not giving information to parents. Individual reports by mothers varied widely, reflecting differences in cases as well as in agency policies. For example, one mother of an emotionally disturbed child said, "The agency holds sessions for parents and helps us on how to behave when the child comes home on weekends." Another mother, whose child was also emotionally disturbed but placed in another agency, said, "I couldn't even get my kid home for Christmas." The placement setting itself brought forth more positive reactions from biological mothers than did the placement agency. The resistance expressed by mothers was not to the child-caring role of agencies, but to the way in which they handled contacts with the families.

In spite of the sense of frustration and powerlessness in solving major problems, the fact that 71 of the 186 mothers reported positive help from agencies in the community should not be ignored. These mothers were ready to name agencies, clinics, and individual social workers whom they reported as being helpful to them. For example, two Black mothers whose children had behavior problems said they got help, one from the Jewish Family Services and the other from the Community Service Society. A white mentally ill mother got help from an AA meeting, a Puerto Rican mother got help from the Family Court, a Black mother from a school social worker, another from the Bureau of Child Guidance, a physically ill Puerto Rican mother from a homemaker sent by the Department of Social Services, and a mentally ill Puerto Rican mother said a social worker from Catholic Charities helped her to work out her problems. These are not dramatic findings, but they are worth noting in view of the plethora of studies reporting poor global outcome from social work services. The individualized and personalized services reported on favorably by many mothers did not take families out of poverty or provide permanent cures, but they did give interim support in a difficult period.

One additional factor reported by respondents as affecting their situations was the passage of time. Nearly half of the mothers said time affected outcome, with 31 percent saying the passage of time helped and 14 percent saying it aggravated problems.

In summary, both personal and agency factors were seen by mothers as affecting their situations to about the same degree. The two major findings are the strong emphasis by respondents on the ways in which they helped themselves, and the fact that one-third of the mothers saw placement agencies as aggravating their situations.

RELATIONSHIP OF STUDY VARIABLES
TO CLIENT RESPONSE

The question was raised as to whether client response to service was related to several of the key study variables, such as ethnic group of client, socioeconomic circumstances, status of placement, and reason for placement. Many differences are seen, some highly significant.

With regard to ethnic group, white mothers reported other persons in their lives as being helpful to a far greater degree than did either Black or Puerto Rican mothers. In terms of the placement agency, Blacks reported a much lower level of help than did either whites or Puerto Ricans. Blacks were also significantly more negative about the placement itself and about contacts with other agencies in the community. Socioeconomic status of mothers was also significantly related to evaluation of intervention efforts, whether by individuals, agencies, or the community. Mothers in the highest socioeconomic group tended to see the child as improving over the years, to see other persons in a positive way, and to regard the placement, as well as other agencies, as significantly more helpful than did mothers of low socioeconomic status.

Whether children were still in care or discharged at the time of the final family interview also affected evaluations. Mothers of children who were at home were more positive about their own roles in improving their situations, and more inclined to see other persons as helpful. They also evaluated the placement agencies in a far more positive light than did mothers whose children were still in care.

When reasons for placement were cross-tabulated by factors affecting intervention, there were significant differences in only two aspects of evaluation. Mothers whose children had been placed for reasons of child behavior saw the child as a more significant actor in their situations, either helping or aggravating matters. In addition, mothers whose children were placed for reasons of neglect and abuse, abandonment, and family dysfunction reported the placement agency as aggravating their problems at a significantly higher level.

The concept of grouping placement reasons as either socially acceptable or socially disapproved was employed at this point. When the four reasons in the acceptable category were grouped together, there were highly significant differences in mothers' responses when compared with those in the disapproved category. Of mothers whose children were placed for acceptable reasons, 71 percent reported other persons in their lives as helpful. This was the case for only 29 percent of the mothers whose children were placed for socially disapproved reasons. Furthermore, 77 percent of mothers in the acceptable category said the placement agency helped, and this was true for only 46 percent of those in the disapproved category. In the latter group, a majority of mothers actually saw the placement agency as aggravating their situations.

Moving from specific foster care agencies to use of broader community resources, the differences between mothers in the two categories persisted at a highly significant level. Of the 186 mothers responding, 70 percent in the acceptable category went voluntarily to community agencies for help. This was true for only 30 percent of mothers whose children were placed for disapproved reasons.

Use of Social Services

The population of families whose children are in foster care tends to be a microcosm of the poverty population in New York City. In addition to being poor, however, these families are unable to carry on their child-caring functions and so become clients of the foster care system. Their involvement with other services, however, shows how interrelated are dependency, health, and child care needs. Of the 186 mothers interviewed five years after placement, 82 percent reported having used services of the Department of Social Services over the placement period, and 73 percent reported using services at a hospital or a clinic for physical illness. In addition, 53 percent of mothers reported having contact with their children's school over special problems, and 39 percent said they used the services of a mental health center or hospital.

The numbers and percentages of mothers in the study sample using various community services (other than foster care) and the percentages of users finding the services helpful, are shown in table 5.

Table 5. Services Used by Mothers in Five Years Since Placement and Percentage of Users Finding Service Helpful (N = 186)

Service	Users		Percentage of Users Finding Service Helpful
	Number	Percent	
Dept. of Social Services	152	82	59
Hospital or Clinic (Physical Illness)	137	73	86
Child's School	99	53	66
Mental Health Center or Hospital	72	39	75
Housing Agency	56	30	32
Legal Aid Agency	45	24	47
Church Group	45	24	71
Job Training	37	20	73
Day Care Center	25	13	80
Community Center	21	11	86
Community Action Group	18	10	72
Social Club or Fraternal Order	7	4	—[a]
Political Group	4	2	—[a]

[a] Numbers too small for useful percentages.

Use of and satisfaction with services did not necessarily go together. For example, the Department of Social Services, the most widely used agency, was reported to be helpful by only 59 percent of users, whereas hospitals and clinics, also heavily utilized, were found to be helpful by 86 percent of clients. Mental hospitals fell between the two, reported as helpful by 75 percent of users. Day-care centers, although not widely used, were considered very helpful by those mothers who had children in them. Least appreciated of all services was the housing agency, reported as helpful by only 32 percent of users. However, when respondents were asked if there was a needed service they did not try to get, housing was widely mentioned. One interpretation suggested by the data is that the poor reports of helpfulness on the part of users of housing agencies was common knowledge, and so persons in need of housing tended to refrain from even trying, assuming that the effort would be fruitless.

In exploring the nature of help received, respondents revealed their own perceptions of services. For example, comments on the help received from the Department of Social Services were almost always about meeting basic needs for food and shelter. Of the 152 respondents who had been clients of the Department of Social Services some time in the five-year study period, only 5 spontaneously mentioned a nonfiscal service. One mother said she was given a better apartment; another said she was helped to budget; another said she learned how to sew; a fourth said she had family counseling; and a fifth reported homemaker service. In response to a specific probe asking if services were received, 18 additional mothers said they had been. However, it is apparent that the department is overwhelmingly perceived by these clients as a source of income support, and not as a resource for meeting total family needs.

The reports of mothers using hospitals and clinics provided information on a wide range of diseases and disabilities. Among the causes for medical care noted by mothers were thyroid conditions, epilepsy, blood clots, diabetes, heart disease, sickle-cell anemia, gall bladder trouble, tuberculosis, kidney trouble, hysterectomies, arthritis, ulcers, and drug addiction. Considering that the median age for mothers at the time of placement was 31 years, these ailments and their prevalence among clients appeared to be far in excess of what would normally be expected for this age group. These data point up the close relationship between need for health care and need for child care, a further argument for an integrated service system.

Mothers were not as specific about complaints and treatment related to visits to mental health centers as they were for hospital visits for physical complaints. Twenty-one mothers, however, said they received psychotherapy. Eight mothers said that they had received medication, and a few said they had received shock treatment. One mother who complained about her experience in a mental health center said, "They tried to sell me a product which I didn't want." This comment was amplified in the interview schedule by the interviewer's note, which explained, "The product was family treatment."

There were 99 mothers who reported on contacts with the child's school over the five-year placement period. Among them was a group of mothers who criticized the educational level, complaining that children weren't taught properly, that classes were too large, and that there were no real efforts at education. Another group of mothers said they were only called to the school to see the teacher when the child was misbehaving, when the marks were bad, and when there were special problems. Approximately one-third of the mothers, however, reported positively on school contacts. The one thing schools did that pleased mothers was telling them about their child's progress in an ongoing way, and not only when there were problems. Typical comments were, "They tell me how he's doing," "I know what's going on." The responses of mothers clearly show that for the school to contact parents only when there is trouble gives an unfortunate connotation to all school-parent relationships. If parents were continuously apprised of the child's progress, they would presumably identify more with the school's efforts both for improvement and problem solution.

Reactions to other services vary. With regard to housing, a minority of mothers expressed satisfaction with getting better apartments, but the majority reported that approaching housing agencies was useless, that you had to wait years for action, that they had made many applications without response, and that in general they felt frustration and despair about even trying to secure satisfactory housing. Job training or employment agency contacts were reported by 37 mothers, of whom 16 said they got jobs. Some of these were from private employment agencies, others from government supported efforts. Several mothers reported additional schooling or training that they hoped would lead them to jobs, and these included a scholarship to a business school from one agency, a high school equivalency diploma, and further on-the-job training.

The ways in which legal aid was used reflect the kinds of problems faced by this group. Mainly, mothers sought help in securing divorces, in having children returned from child care agencies, in bringing suits against landlords, and in getting help when a family member was in trouble with the law.

Day care, used by only 13 percent of the mothers, was reported as being a helpful service, but not primarily for the reason that might be expected, i.e., to enable mothers to work. Mothers said day care was useful because it let them shop, gave babysitting help, helped when they were not well enough to watch children, and took children off the street and provided supervision. These reasons reflect the fact that most of these mothers are essentially not in the labor market, and had had mental and physical disabilities which limited child-caring functions. Thus day care is seen as helping mothers to resume child care rather than helping them to take on jobs.[1]

Community centers and settlement houses were reported by mothers as helping to keep children off the streets, as sending them to camp, and as helping with disciplinary problems. Community action groups were seen as having a broader impact, including help with getting jobs, help with welfare rights, and help with housing suits. One mother stated that community action groups were not very helpful because (referring to Vietnam) "The war is still on despite their demands."

Only 4 mothers said activity in a political group was helpful. By the 45 mothers who reported utilizing church groups, there was a generally high level of appreciation of spiritual leadership, family counseling, and concrete services. A few mothers mentioned bingo as their main source of satisfaction. Where dissatisfaction with church groups was expressed, it tended to relate to the fact that the church did not take the client's children into parochial schools.

An analysis was made of whether there was differential use of services by the study population according to ethnic group, socioeco-

---

[1] Jenkins and Sauber found that in a sample of 894 families with children in foster care, only 5 percent reported any experience with day care. Shirley Jenkins and Mignon Sauber, *Paths to Child Placement, Family Situations Prior to Foster Care* (New York: Community Council of Greater New York, Inc., 1966).

nomic status, placement reason, and current status of the placement (whether the child was in care or had been discharged). A number of significant differences emerged. With regard to ethnic group, there were significant differences in use of services in 6 separate categories. Assistance from the Department of Social Services was received by 96 percent of all Puerto Rican mothers, 80 percent of Blacks, and 64 percent of whites. The same groupings were seen for hospital services, used by 83 percent of Puerto Ricans, 71 percent of Blacks, and 64 percent of whites. On the other hand, a different pattern was seen with regard to use of schools, legal aid, and church groups. In these cases, whites and Puerto Ricans tended to use services, while Blacks were very low users. Only 16 percent of Black respondents said they had sought legal aid. Only 40 percent of Black mothers said they had had contact with the school, and only 12 percent said they had had contact with church groups. Blacks also reported lower levels of contact with mental health clinics.

Variables other than ethnicity were related to use of services in a few instances. As would be expected, mothers in the lowest socioeconomic group predominated as clients of the Department of Social Services. They were also the major group seeking aid in housing. Physical health facilities were used most extensively by those mothers in the lowest socioeconomic group, mental health facilities by those in the highest socioeconomic group. Mothers whose children had been discharged reported significantly more involvement with church groups and community action centers than did mothers whose children were still in placement.

Certain findings emerge from this review of use of specific services. From the demographic data obtained from home interviews, it was obvious that the mothers comprised a poverty group, and it would be expected that concrete services directly related to income maintenance would be used. The almost universal use of hospitals and clinics and the extensive health needs of the mothers were also highlighted by the data on services. Of interest was the significantly low level of use of certain services reported by Black mothers in contrast to the high use by both whites and Puerto Ricans. This finding has clear ethnic implications, and leads to many questions about the way Black mothers perceive community agencies, including schools, legal aid, and mental health services. The other unanswered question is whether the agencies welcome Black clients, and whether differential services are offered.

In order to probe further client perceptions of service delivery, three attitudinal questions were asked. They were:

1. In your opinion, is there a difference between an agency run by a private organization and one run by a city or government? If yes, what is the difference and which do you prefer?
2. Does it make a difference if the people who run an agency are of the same ethnic group as the client? In what ways?
3. Does it make a difference if the people who run an agency are of the same religious group as the client? In what ways?

In response to the first question, fewer than half of the mothers, 40 percent, said it did not matter whether an agency was under public or voluntary auspices, and 16 percent were ambivalent. Of the rest, 33 percent preferred private auspices and 11 percent preferred government auspices. Mothers who saw no difference between the public and private agency expressed both positive and negative reactions to services. On the positive side, some of the comments were, "They all try to help you," and "It depends on the person you get—on the worker, not on the agency." One mother said, "I am broadminded, help is help." Negative reactions ran along the following lines; "If you have no money, they're all hard on you"; "It's hard to say, I've had my difficulties with both"; and "They are all so busy, neither one has time for you."

The mothers who preferred agencies under private or voluntary auspices almost all said that private agencies had more time for the client, cared more for people, and gave what professionals would call individualized services. One mother after another said, "They have more respect for the person"; "They are more dedicated"; "They are more confidential"; "They take a more personal interest"; "They take more time with you." When clients preferred the public agency, on the other hand, the reason given was that public agencies had more money and could help financially. Negative comments on the public agencies were: "They have more investigation"; "They are too big, they pay no attention to the individual"; "They are always checking up on you"; "It's hard to get your child back from them, it is easier from the private agency"; "People who work for the government are too lazy." One mother said, "They are too cold. I had to visit my child in a hallway. My friend who has a child with a private agency visited in a room with a sofa and with toys."

It was apparent that clients were not fully aware of the ways in which purchase of care operated, or the extent to which public funds supported the voluntary services. Their responses were directed to the nature of the personal contacts. Government was seen as cold, impersonal, moneyed but not interested in the individual. When respondents were analyzed in terms of socioeconomic group, there was relatively stronger preference for private agencies on the part of the higher socioeconomic group. In terms of reason for placement, the preference was especially strong for mothers with children placed for emotional disturbance.

The responses show that the desire of mothers for individualized services and for a sense that workers express personal interest in their problems is very strong. Whether their perceptions of differences in this regard between public and voluntary agencies reflect actual differences in practice is not at issue here. What is clear is that the desire of clients for individualized services is a major concern.

There was little support among the respondents for the proposition that ethnic or religious auspices of an agency made a difference to them. Over 80 percent of mothers said it did not, and there was almost no ambivalence expressed. When these overall responses were examined in terms of some relevant variables, however, some significant differences did emerge. The strongest support for ethnic composition of agencies came from the Puerto Rican mothers: 23 percent of them, as compared with 11 percent of whites and 10 percent of Blacks, said it made a difference. The reason given specifically related to communication—having a Spanish-speaking worker who understands what is said. One mother interviewed in Spanish said, "I can't even say 'Yes' in English."

There were only 8 Black mothers who said that the ethnic correspondence of the agency did make a difference to them, but the spontaneous comments of 7 of them were not in the expected direction. The tenor was that Blacks don't help their own people as they should, that Black workers are less sympathetic, and, as one woman said, "The whites get you more money, the Blacks cut you back." One Black mother, however, said she would prefer a Black worker because "White women don't give you a chance to tell them anything." A special analysis was made of ethnic correspondence of respondent and interviewer, to see if this affected responses. Of the 64 Black mothers who answered this question, 42 had Black interviewers and 22 had white interviewers. Of those Black mothers who said it made a difference, in a prowhite direction, 4 had Black interviewers and 3 had white interviewers. The numbers are too few to generalize, but ethnic correspondence did not appear to affect responses.

Responses from the majority of mothers who said that ethnic correspondence was not important tended to fall into two main categories. About half of the mothers spoke of their own lack of prejudice, with such answers as, "All people are the same"; "If people help you, it doesn't matter what they look like"; and "I have no prejudice, I treat all alike." The other half stressed the importance of the professional competence of the worker. They made such comments as, "The important thing is if they are professionals"; "They are trained to do a job"; "It doesn't matter as long as they do their job."

With regard to religious affiliation, about the same kinds of responses were given, but with some differences in terms of religious group of respondent. Jewish and Catholic mothers tended to want religious correspondence to a greater extent than did Protestant mothers. Specific reasons given by Catholic mothers related to their wish to have their children placed in Catholic settings and given Catholic upbringings.

These data need to be interpreted with caution. There is a substantial literature on the issue of ethnic correspondence in service delivery, on development of ethnic agencies, and on matching of interviewer and respondent in terms of study methodology. Brieland studied preference of Blacks in relation to race of service givers, using both Black and white interviewers.[2] The findings showed that Black clients preferred to receive services from Blacks, given equal training and competence. Furthermore, the strength of this response was greater if the interviewer was Black. Ethnicity, however, is not the only variable in the worker-client relationship—class and status are also involved. In a study of the validity of interview responses on the part of welfare mothers, when both interviewers and respondents were Black, Weiss investigated the effects of social distance and status.[3] She found that bias was associated with high rapport and status similarity between interviewer and respondent. Lower levels of rapport but higher validity were found where there were status differences, even though all parties corresponded in ethnicity.

The mothers with children in foster care had experienced acute problems of both dependency and child care. They relied heavily on agency services for meeting their needs. They were responding to the question on ethnic correspondence in terms of their own experiences in the service delivery system, rather than some idealized model. Issues of status and class differences, and public and private sponsorship are all intermingled with those of ethnic correspondence, and probably account for the responses given.

[2] Donald Brieland, "Black Identity and the Helping Person," *Children,* 16, No. 5 (1969), 170–76.

[3] Carol Weiss, "Validity of Welfare Mothers' Interview Responses," *Public Opinion Quarterly,* 32 (1968–69), 622–33.

Early Help and Primary Prevention

To further describe client perceptions of help, two additional questions, one on early intervention and one on primary prevention were asked. They were: "What would have helped at the time of placement," and "What might have prevented your problems—in other words made your life different so your problems might never have existed."

On early intervention, clients were presented with a checklist of eight possible kinds of help, and were asked to indicate which three would have made the most difference. Among the first three choices of items on the list, the strongest response was "More money"; second was "Help from my family"; and third was, "Help from a social worker." These were followed by references to homemaker help, better housing, and better health. Day care was low on the list. There were some interesting differences by study variables. For example, the greatest expressions of need for homemakers were from the lowest socioeconomic group, from Black mothers, and from mothers whose children had been placed because of their own physical illness. Help from one's own family was reported as needed by 56 percent of Black mothers, 44 percent of white mothers, and 34 percent of Puerto Ricans.

Moving to primary prevention, there were three important groups of reasons developed from the spontaneous responses of the mothers. The first group, reported by 44 percent of mothers, refers to the father of the children, whether or not he was the legal spouse. Comments by mothers ranged from "If I only had not gotten married in the first place" to "If I had the courage to throw my husband out" to "Maybe I should have stayed with my husband for the children's sake." There were several references to husbands who were addicts and to the fact that drugs had destroyed family life. One mother said "I should have married my own kind—a Jamaican instead of a Greek."

The second reference, given by 41 percent of mothers, said things would have been different if their own family history had been different. Here the mother was reporting about her own parents, her upbringing, or certain earlier problems in family life. Some of these references related to separation and some to damage. One mother said "If I hadn't been brought up as a foster child." Another one said "It was my mother who ruined my life—what a mother does to a child is a shame." A third said, "My mother's husband forced sex on me when I was a child—I told her but she didn't believe me." The reactions to own family life, as well as to life with the spouse, are not in all one direction. There is no idealizing here of family life. In some cases there is a poignant sense of deprivation due to separation from own parents, in other cases there is strong anger and hostility at having been with parents and experienced violence and neglect.

The next group of proposals for primary prevention reported by from 15 to 40 percent of mothers in each subcategory related to environmental situations, such as poverty, housing, education, migration, family planning, jobs, discrimination, and health. One mother said, "If I had been a millionaire." Several referred to housing problems, saying "If I had a safe place to live." Another said "If I had a house with a yard—my child fell from the fire escape and it was terrible." One mother said "If I had a high school diploma I would have been all right." Health needs referred not so much to health care as to devastating diseases, such as, "If they had a way to cure sickle-cell anemia." Or "If they knew how to properly diagnose brain damage." Migration issues were stated primarily by Puerto Ricans, including comments such as, "If I had been born in New York and not Puerto Rico," or "If I had stayed in Puerto Rico." One mother said "I should have stayed in Italy." Perhaps the mother who went furthest back in primary prevention was the one who said, "If my Indian ancestors hadn't had their land taken away from them."

Perceptions Summary

On the basis of the study findings, a guarded answer can be given to the question raised in the beginning of this chapter, "Does the 'help' help?" The answer is "Sometimes and in some ways." An important finding is that two-thirds of all mothers saw self-help as being the primary positive factor in making things better. Only half said that other persons had helped them, a third said that others had made things worse. Relatives were often condemned, and the stereotype of the extended family as a ready resource is not applicable for most of these families. The placement agency was also seen as aggravating problems in one-third of cases, and received fewer positive perceptions from mothers than did the child-caring facility.

The most positive feelings about agency operations were in relation to individualized and personalized services. As a group, the mothers in the highest socioeconomic group used more services, and perceived them as more helpful. There were significant differences in response to service between mothers with children placed for socially acceptable reasons and those with children placed for disapproved reasons, supporting a main thesis of this study that there is less use of services by those in greatest need.

In terms of specific services used, there were two main findings. One was the extensive need for hospital and clinic services for this population, reflecting the relationship of dependency and health needs to placement. Also of importance is the ethnic analysis, which shows lower use of many services, aside from income maintenance and health, by Black families. Although money and health were seen by most families as their main needs at the time of placement, when asked about primary prevention mothers in the study reached into their own family lives, and related interpersonal factors as being responsible for their early problems. Of lesser importance in their responses were references by the mothers to social factors affecting their life situations. Their perceptions were sharp, but narrowly focused.

Six

Role
Expectations
of Mothers
as Clients

Client perceptions of foster care and of community services have been discussed in the two preceding chapters. Another dimension of this analysis involves mothers' perceptions of what is expected of them by agency workers and what they expect of themselves.

These perceptions have important practice implications. Work with mothers whose children are in care can be facilitated when the worker comprehends the behavioral expectations the client attaches to her role. Briar and Miller, for example, state:

The caseworker, if he is to be perceived as helpful by the client, must minimize discrepancies between his own and his client's conception of what they are doing together. To do so requires that the caseworker make an effort to discover his client's conceptions and expectations and be prepared, accordingly, to modify his own behavior and his expectations of the client or else educate the client to the worker's views.[1]

[1] Scott Briar and Henry Miller, *Problems and Issues in Social Casework* (New York: Columbia University Press, 1971), p. 109.

Role expectations, called norms by some social scientists,[2] prescriptions by others,[3] refer to a set of specifications for role-appropriate behavior, or ideas of what people think behavior ought to be with respect to a specific position in a social system. In this study, the concern is with role expectations of biological mothers with children in placement when they are involved in face-to-face interviews with caseworkers from child-caring agencies.

The data on role expectations were collected in the second family study interview conducted during 1968. At that time 243 mothers were interviewed, of whom 136 had children still in placement. The sample for the study of role expectations was limited to these 136 mothers, since the remaining 107 mothers, whose children had been discharged from care, would have been responding on the basis of recall rather than from ongoing experience. Their reactions would therefore be less valid than those of mothers with children currently in care. Of the 136, responses could not be secured in 8 cases, so that the response sample for analysis contained 128 cases.

The Role Questions

Two series of questions intended to elicit role expectations were included in the interview. One group of questions asked how the study mothers felt they were expected to behave when they were with the placement agency caseworkers. The questions were:

During a face-to-face talk (visit) with the agency caseworker, how do you think she expects you to behave (act)? What things would she expect you to do or say? What things would she expect you not to do or say?

A second group of questions asked how the mothers expected themselves to behave in such circumstances. The questions were:

[2] George C. Homans, *The Human Group* (New York: Harcourt, Brace, Jovanovich, 1950).

[3] Bruce Biddle and Edwin J. Thomas, *Role Theory: Concepts and Research* (New York: Wiley, 1966).

How do you yourself feel you should behave (act) in a talk (visit) with an agency caseworker? What things do you feel you should do or say? What things do you feel you should not do or say?

Numerous research studies have utilized various methods of obtaining data on behavioral expectations other than the open type of interview question used in this study. In an attempt to derive the role expectations of Mexican and American students, for example, Nall used responses to contructed stories.[4] Wispé used lists of items reflecting desirable traits to ascertain expectations for insurance salesmen.[5] Forty-three statements describing the type of behavior expected of ministers was used in a study by Bentz.[6] Role playing and sentence completion were employed by Thomas, Polansky, and Kounin in deriving data on the expected behavior of persons in the "helping" professions.[7] In this study, however, direct questioning of mothers was considered preferable to other methods. Role playing was impossible within the limits of the interview situation, where extensive additional data were being collected; and essay writing was impractical, considering the educational background of the group. Constructed stories, checklists of traits, adjectives or statements based on an outsider's a priori inferences as to expected role behavior seemed less likely to produce valid data than respondents' unstructured expression of ideas, feelings, and perceptions. Furthermore, the person-to-person interviewing context allowed for follow-up and probing by interviewers in order to clarify ambiguous or unclear statements, a further argument in favor of the direct, open type of questioning. It should be noted, however, that interviewers reported that respondents found the

[4] F. C. Nall II, "Role Expectations: A Cross-Cultural Study," *Rural Sociology,* 27 (1962), 28–41.

[5] L. G. A. Wispé, "A Sociometric Analysis of Conflicting Role Expectancies," *American Journal of Sociology,* 61 (1955), 134–37.

[6] W. Kenneth Bentz, "Consensus between Role Expectations and Role Behavior among Ministers," *Community Mental Health Journal,* 4 (August 1968), 301–306.

[7] Edwin Thomas, Norman Polansky, and Jacob Kounin, "The Expected Behavior of a Potentially Helpful Person," *Human Relations,* 8, No. 2 (1955), 165–74.

role questions difficult to answer, and there were many cases in which the questions had to be repeated several times. It was to be expected that it would be difficult to respond to a question that involved putting oneself in the place of another. With patience and time, however, interviewers did elicit meaningful answers from all but the 8 respondents excluded from the sample.

The Role Expectations

The mothers' spontaneous responses to the questions fell into five distinct categories. These were developed on an ad-hoc basis after every interview was read and studied. The categories were mutually exclusive in terms of each response given, but since mothers could give multiple replies to the role questions, it was possible for the different replies of any one mother to fit into several expectation categories.

Three members of the research staff participated as judges in coding the categories for the role expectation responses. Every case was coded by two judges. Where a difference occurred a third judge was consulted for a decision. Differences occurred between the two original judges in the coding of only 14 percent of the expectations; these differences were resolved in favor of one judge in 52 percent of the cases and the other judge in 48 percent.

The five categories of role expectations were as follows:

1. To be undisguised.
2. To be controlled.
3. To display concern for the child.
4. To be formal.
5. To be acquiescent.

Each of the expectations will be described in turn in the order of frequency in which they were mentioned.

To be undisguised. This expectation had several dimensions, each conveying a sense of obligation to be undefended, overt, expressive, unconcealed, and comprehensive about events, experiences, and conscious emotional feelings. Since the mothers' relationships with the workers differed, the content and direction of the verbalizations of this expectation also differed, but the same essential meaning was conveyed by all responses coded in this category.

The expectation was sometimes phrased simply as a requirement to be honest and frank. The mothers made such statements as: "I should not tell lies or be dishonest"; "I should tell the truth"; "Don't pretend"; "Be honest, truthful, don't hide or deliberately lie"; "Don't color anything for them"; "Be frank." At other times the expectation was stated as a requirement to be "natural," "normal," "relaxed," "The same as I do any other time."

Most often, however, the expectation was expressed in terms of an obligation to be candid and open. In a talk with the agency caseworkers the mothers felt they should: "Say whatever comes to my mind"; "Tell her everything"; "Sometimes you say what you do not want to say and that's what they want to hear"; "I should say what I feel"; "Not be afraid to express feelings"; "Get excited, scream"; "Talk freely"; "Not hold back"; "Talk about things that annoy me"; "Talk about intimacies"; "Talk about my doubts"; "Talk about my husband's cruelty."

To be controlled. Here the mothers conveyed their perceptions that in their relationships with the workers they felt obliged to hold back verbal or active expression of feelings, particularly angry and hostile feelings, and to exclude a wide range of topics from conversation. They considered themselves obliged to be controlled, censored, and to hold a tight rein on their feelings.

One way the mothers phrased this expectation was as a requirement to contain anger, hostility, disruptive behavior, and bad language in the presence of the worker. They made statements saying they should: "Not get excited or upset"; "Not be angry"; "Not act up or make a scene"; "Get hold of myself, control myself"; "Not show anger or curse her"; "Not create unpleasant scenes"; "Not yell or raise my voice"; "Don't use foul language"; "Not act violent"; "Not hit them"; "Not put her through a wall."

Another aspect of this expectation that mothers expressed was a need to exclude certain subjects from their talks with workers, particularly topics about themselves or their feelings. In contacts with the caseworker, mothers said they should: "Not tell her my personal problems"; "Not involve them in things that are personal like my husband"; "Not tell private things"; "Not trouble her about my own problems"; "Don't tell anything confidential"; "Not complain about foster mother"; "Not talk against the foster mother"; "Not say the bad part, show everything is good."

To display concern for the child. This general expectation conveyed the obligation felt by the mothers to prove to the workers that they were concerned about their children. They felt they were expected to indicate interest in their children in some way, whether it be by asking about how they are getting along—their health, schoolwork, friends, behavior—by asking for the discharge of the children, by pressing for more frequent visits, or by expressing affection for the children.

In this context, the following statements were made: (I should) "Be an interested mother"; "Be concerned about the kids"; "Ask how the children are doing, getting along"; "Talk about the child's progress"; "Ask how he behaves"; "Talk about child's problems, school, health"; "Ask to take children home"; "Say I'm taking my child home"; "Be eager to get child back"; "Let them know you want your children"; "Visit regularly"; "Ask to visit child"; "Promise to visit the child"; "Want to hold the baby"; "Show love to the boy"; "Show affection for the child."

To be formal. This general expectation conveys a requirement to behave in a reserved, distant, and polite manner. It includes the idea of courteousness and good manners, with limited involvement. Some examples of the mothers' statements regarding this expectation follow. They said they should: "Be nice and polite"; "Behave well"; "Be polite and formal"; "Be well-mannered"; "Be polite"; "Treat her cordially"; "Be reserved"; "Behave properly"; "Act like a lady"; "Be friendly"; "Not be rude"; "Act courteous, well-mannered"; The expectation "to be formal" differs from "to be controlled" in that the former is actually a positive action to behave in a way that is mutually approved. The latter is an inhibition of action, in which unacceptable and disapproved behavior is held back but the negative aspects are well recognized by the respondent.

To be acquiescent. This category implied acceptance of worker's decisions with regard to themselves and their children, and cooperation with workers by giving all requested information. In addition, not pressing for discharge of the child or for more frequent visits with the child was considered to convey the concept of the expectation, "to be acquiescent." Statements such as those that follow were made. One should: "Not run their business"; "Accept what they say"; "Listen to her"; "Not interfere in their plans"; "Don't interfere with her authority"; "Work with them, not tell them what to do"; "Be cooperative"; "Answer all their questions"; "Give necessary information"; "Not push for unrealistic action"; "Not pressure to get the child back"; "Not ask for extra visiting hours"; "Have patience."

FREQUENCY AND COMMONALITY OF RESPONSES

Each mother who participated in the interview gave two sets of responses, one referring to her perception of behavioral expectations of caseworkers and another to her own expectations for herself. In the categories of "undisguised," "controlled," and "concerned," for about half the mothers expectations for caseworkers and self were the same. This was the case for about one third of the mothers giving "formal" and one fourth giving "acquiescent" responses. The major differences in perceptions were in three categories: being controlled and being formal were expressed more frequently as an expectation for oneself, and being acquiescent as what the caseworker expected.

The analysis of role-behavior expectations in relation to other study variables will be made for the combined responses in relation to both workers and self. In addition to responding to two sets of questions, mothers could give multiple responses to each of these sets. There was high variability in the numbers of responses each mother gave, some giving one and some giving ten or more to each set. To avoid too much fragmentation and numbers too small to analyze, it was decided to group responses to both question sets together and treat them as the role expectations of the mother in the situational context. Using the combined responses as a base, and including multiple answers, "undisguised" was mentioned most frequently by mothers, followed by "controlled" and "concerned." "Formal" and "acquiescent" were next, and were mentioned in equal numbers.

Role Expectations and Study Variables

After the five main expressed role expectations had been determined, the next task was to investigate whether they were related to other key study variables. Ten such variables were included in the analysis. Three reflect institutional arrangements in the foster care system: type of placement, size of agency, and sectarian auspices of agency. Two variables reflect the interaction between mother and worker: the topics discussed and the number of contacts. The next two variables relate to demographic data on mothers: ethnic group and socioeconomic level. The final three variables reflect attitudes of mothers. Three indexes were developed to measure: maternal commitment to the child; maternal motivation for role incumbency—respondents' readiness to become mothers with children in care—based on perceptions of necessity for placement; and mothers' evaluations of the foster care system.

TYPE OF PLACEMENT, SIZE OF AGENCY, AND KIND OF AUSPICES

Of the 128 mothers responding to the questions on role expectations, 47 percent had children in foster family care, 14 percent in residential treatment centers, and 39 percent in other institutional settings. Two sets of responses were significantly associated with type of placement.

All but one of the mothers with children in residential treatment stated that their role expectation was to be "undisguised." This almost universal response is understandable in terms of the treatment experience and of the work undertaken with families. The second statistically significant response was the finding that mothers with children in foster family care were more likely to perceive "controlled" as their behavioral expectation than were mothers with children in treatment centers or institutions. These data seem to reinforce the earlier finding in which mothers reported problems and frustrations in visiting children when they were in foster family homes, and role conflicts with foster mothers. The control response may be related to the way in which they have learned to cope with that situation.

Numerous studies have found that the conceptions people have of their roles in relation to social service agencies vary according to the size of the organizational unit. Thomas, for example, found that in small organizations there was a greater compatibility of role conceptions and greater role consensus than in larger organizations.[8] To explore this area, mothers' behavioral expectations were analyzed in terms of the size of the child-caring agencies.

The most relevant basis for measuring size was the total number of children for which an agency was responsible. Three categories were established: small agencies, caring for 250 or fewer children; medium-sized agencies, caring for from 251 to 500 children; and large agencies who had over 500 children in care. Of the 128 families in this sample, 27 percent of children were in small, 25 percent in medium, and 48 percent in large agencies at the time the mothers were interviewed.

The analysis of data shows significant differences in three categories of behavioral expectation. "To be undisguised," the category reflecting openness and communication, was expressed to a sig-

[8] Edwin J. Thomas, "Role Conceptions and Organizational Size," *American Sociological Review,* 24, No. 1 (February 1959) 30–37.

nificantly greater extent by mothers with children in small agencies. On the other hand, mothers with children in large agencies tended to see their appropriate roles as expressing concern for the child and being acquiescent to the caseworker. These findings, however, cannot be interpreted only in terms of organizational size but must be related to the kind of care given. The majority of residential treatment centers were small, and the majority of foster family agencies were large. Thus the association already noted between behavioral expectations and type of placement is reinforced by and may even be reflected in the analysis of size of agency.

The New York City foster care system operates primarily through purchase of care from voluntary agencies, supplemented by public facilities. Furthermore, there is a legal obligation in New York State to give preference, where practicable, to placing children with an agency whose sponsorship is by those of the same religious faith as that of the child's family.[9] This preferential placement is not operable for nonsectarian private agencies, nor, obviously, for agencies in the public sector. Nevertheless, the majority of children in placement in New York City have been cared for by agencies primarily sponsored by persons of their own religion.[10] This was the case for the 128 mothers answering the role expectation questions. Three-quarters of the children of Catholic and Jewish families were in placement in

[9] The legal status of this provision was challenged in a brief known as *Wilder vs. Sugarman*. It was submitted jointly by the New York Civil Liberties Union and the Legal Aid Society as a class action on behalf of destitute, dependent, and neglected New York City children who had been in need of care outside of their homes, but who were allegedly denied needed services. The claim was that the purchase of child welfare services from voluntary sectarian agencies resulted in a system that discriminated against Black Protestant children. The arguments were heard before the federal district court, who rejected the suit and upheld the right of the foster care agencies to receive support despite the constitutional prohibition of state aid to religion. Left to a further court proceeding was the issue of specific application, and whether plaintiffs were deprived of their First Amendment or other federal constitutional rights. (See *New York Times,* July 21 and November 20, 1974.)

[10] Frances Kroll, *Perspectives on Foster Care in New York City* (New York: Child Welfare Research Program, Columbia University School of Social Work, June 1967), p. 9.

agencies of their own faith, but only half of the children of Protestant families were placed in Protestant-sponsored agencies. One-third of the children of Protestant families were being cared for by the public agencies.

The data show that mothers with children in agencies under Jewish auspices were significantly more likely to mention being "undisguised" as their appropriate role expectation. Mothers of children in Protestant agencies tended to mention control, and mothers of children in Catholic agencies to mention formality as their major behavioral expectation. Those mothers with children in nonsectarian agencies tended to report their major expectations as "to express concern for the child," and "to be acquiescent toward the worker."

The association between the variable of religious auspices and the perceived role expectations can be explained in part through the interrelationship with the two other organizational variables already discussed, type of placement and size of agency. The majority of Jewish foster care agencies in the study were residential treatment centers, whereas the Protestant agencies tended to offer foster home care. It is not surprising, therefore, to find the expectation "undisguised" related to Jewish agency auspices, and "controlled" to Protestant agency auspices. Religious auspices and size of agency are also related. The majority of nonsectarian agencies were large, and the responses of "concern" and "acquiescent" were expressed for both of these variables. Thus the three organizational variables tend to be associated both with each other and with perceived role expectations.

MOTHER-WORKER INTERACTION

There is a wide range of topics that conceivably could be discussed in the caseworker-mother interview. An appropriate question is whether the kinds of subjects talked about were associated with the behavioral expectations of mothers.

In response to the question, "In a face-to-face talk with the agency caseworker, what would you talk about?" all the interviewed mothers mentioned one or more of the following subject areas: (1) discussion of the child's activities and progress in placement (i.e., "We would talk about how my child was doing in foster care, how he was getting along"); (2) discussion of practical arrangements concerning visiting the child in placement or discharge of the child to his home (i.e., "We would discuss visiting arrangements to see my child," or "Things like what was standing in the way of his coming home"); and (3) discussion of the mothers as individuals, their life situations and personal problems (i.e., "We would talk about me, my problems, how things were for me"). Seventy-three percent of the mothers said they talked about how the child was doing in placement, 24 percent mentioned talking about discharge or visiting and 36 percent said they talked about themselves.[11]

Women who said they talked about themselves with the caseworker also mentioned the role expectation "to be undisguised" to a significantly greater extent than did other women. Mothers who stressed talking about their child with the worker were those who perceived their expected role behavior to be expressing "concern for the child." Finally, discharge and/or visiting of the child were likely to be topics of conversation among women who had control or acquiescence as their role expectations.

The number of personal, face-to-face contacts mothers of the placed children have with their caseworkers is mainly determined by the agency, rather than by the mother. Although a mother may on occasion initiate appointments, and may also refuse interviews or not appear for them, on the whole it is worker's initiative that determines the contacts. The average number of personal contacts of the 128 mothers with their caseworkers during the six months preceding the study interview was 3.5, or somewhat more than once every two months. Twenty-five percent of the women had not seen a worker at all during the six-month period, and 7 percent had seen a worker 12 times or more (at least twice a month). When analyzed in terms of the categories of behavioral expectation, those mothers who stressed the

[11] Mothers could mention more than one topic, hence the total exceeds 100 percent.

need "to express concern for the child" and "to be controlled" saw their caseworkers somewhat less frequently than others. The differences, however, were not statistically significant.

DEMOGRAPHIC DATA: ETHNIC GROUP AND SOCIOECONOMIC CIRCUMSTANCES

Throughout the study, demographic factors were major distinguishing variables in the data analysis. The analysis of role expectations was no exception. With regard to ethnic group, of the 128 mothers in this sample, 27 percent were white, 43 percent were Black, and 30 percent were Puerto Rican. Significantly more white women than others mentioned being "undisguised" as representing their role expectation. Puerto Rican women reported "to be formal" as a role expectation significantly more than did others. Black mothers tended to mention "to be controlled" and "to be acquiescent" as reflecting their role expectations. Mothers of minority groups, i.e., Blacks and Puerto Ricans together, tended to "express concern for the child" more frequently than did whites.

The analysis of role expectations in relation to socioeconomic circumstances of families in the study produced results that were not unexpected. Significantly more high-status women mentioned "undisguised," and significantly more middle- and low-status women mentioned "concern for the child." Women of low status tended to mention control and acquiescence as major behavioral expectations. These findings can be interpreted partly in terms of the interrelationships of the variables. For example, both type of placement and ethnic group are related to socioeconomic circumstances. A further factor, however, may be the level of communication between client and worker.

In a British study of client reactions, Mayer and Timms found that "clients assumed that only persons who had a similar experience could possibly comprehend [them]. . . . They typically preferred workers of the same age, marital status, and sex as themselves. Being similar [such workers] would understand what they, the clients had been through." [12] The caseworkers in the New York City foster care system differed considerably in ethnic group and socioeconomic level from the mothers they served. Although no separate analysis has been done of characteristics of the workers for the 128 mothers whose perceptions are reported here, for all families in the study caseworkers were found to be 76 percent white, 15 percent Black, and the remainder of Spanish, Asian, or other backgrounds. [13] Furthermore, by the nature of their job descriptions, all were college graduates. Although there was a wide educational and income gap between the white mothers in high socioeconomic circumstances and the caseworkers, relative to other mothers in the study this was the smallest gap in overall demographic variables. Thus the propensity of white mothers of high socioeconomic level to mention the role expectation "undisguised," and that of nonwhite, low-socioeconomic-level mothers to note the more constrained role expectations of control and formality, might also reflect the degree of correspondence (or lack of it) between each group and its workers.

MATERNAL COMMITMENT, MOTIVATION, AND EVALUATION OF THE SYSTEM

The extent to which an individual is committed to or identifies with an assumed role can influence perceptions of behavioral expectations attached to that role. Goffman has noted that, rather than with attachment and commitment, many roles can be played with detachment, shame, and resentment. He used the term "role distance" to label the expressed detachment of the performer from his role. Goffman discusses the distinction between the concepts of attachment and commitment, noting that a mother is "attached" to that role simply by virtue of the fact that she bears a child, but that does not necessarily make her "committed" to the role of mother. Potential adoptive parents, for

[12] John E. Mayer and Noel Timms, *The Client Speaks, Working Class Impressions of Casework* (New York: Atherton Press, 1970), p. 73.

[13] Deborah Shapiro, *Agencies and Children: A Child Welfare Network's Investment in its Clients* (New York: Columbia University Press, forthcoming), chapter 2.

example, may be "committed" to the parental role while not yet "attached" to it. The woman who has borne the child that these adoptive parents will take is "attached" to the role of mother but seemingly not "committed" to it.[14]

In order to obtain some measure of maternal commitment to relate to role expectations an index was constructed using responses to four relevant questions asked during the study interview. These covered: (1) the frequency of visits by the mother to the placed child, (2) whether the mother reported taking care of a child as a positive or negative task, (3) whether or not the mother worried about the child while in placement, and (4) whether or not the mother included the child in her plans for the coming year. In combination, the responses to these questions were designated as a role commitment index.

The data on frequency of visits were derived from mothers' reports on how often they had seen their children since placement.[15] These responses are based on recall, and thus susceptible to error. They were grouped into three categories, based on frequency of visits. The categories included mothers who reported visiting less than once a month, 30 percent; those visiting once a month but less than twice, 20 percent; and those visiting twice a month or more, 43 percent. No answer was obtained for this question from the remaining 7 percent. There are certain limitations on using frequency of visiting as a measure of maternal commitment, since some mothers could not visit often because of physical or mental illness, the expense of the visit to distant placements, or restrictions on visiting imposed by workers or agency policy. In many cases, however, it did reflect mothers' involvement with children, and it therefore was used as one of four of the variables in the commitment index.

During the research interviews each of the mothers was asked

[14] Erving Goffman, *Encounters, Two Studies in the Sociology of Interaction* (Indianapolis, Indiana: Bobbs-Merrill, 1961), pp. 85–115.

[15] These data vary somewhat from visiting reports of the overall study sample, as noted in chapter 4. They refer to visiting patterns of the 128 mothers with children still in care at the time of the second field interview.

to complete the open-ended sentence, "Taking care of a child is . . ." Their answers were coded into three categories, negative responses (i.e., "a burden," "a big responsibility"), positive responses (i.e., "a joy," "happiness," "God's work"), or a combination of both (i.e., "enjoyable and difficult"). Fifty-six percent of the women responded negatively, 30 percent positively, 9 percent both positively and negatively, and no answer was obtained from the remaining 5 percent. The attitude toward child care reflected by these answers was included as the second variable of the role commitment index.

Each mother was asked if she worried about how her child was getting along in foster care placement. Fifty-three percent of the women indicated they did worry, 44 percent indicated they did not worry, and 3 percent did not answer the question. Worry about how the child was faring in a strange setting away from home was considered to be an appropriate reaction, and a relevant variable to include in the measure of maternal role commitment.

Close to the end of the research interview each woman was asked, "What are your plans for next year?" In the spontaneous responses 39 percent of mothers included the placed children in their plans for the coming year, 19 percent said they had no plans at all, 38 percent mentioned plans but did not include their child, and 4 percent did not answer the question. Inclusion of the child in the spontaneous answer to this nondirective question was considered to be an indication of role commitment on the part of the respondent and was utilized as the fourth variable in the index.

Each of the four variables included was ranked in three categories. The most negative category was coded rank 1; the most positive, rank 3; and the middle category, coded rank 2, was reserved for mixed, indecisive, or ambivalent answers. An individual's commitment index score was calculated by adding scores on all four variables. Potential scores therefore ranged from 4 to 12, with 4 representing very low maternal commitment and 12 representing very high commitment. The average study mother scored 7.9 on the index.

There was no evidence that any of the four included variables was more significant than any other as an indicator of maternal commitment, and therefore they received equal weight in the index. To secure some indication of the effect of the variables, correlations were obtained between each of them and the combined index. The results showed correlation coefficients ranging from .50 to .55, indicating that no one variable was dominant.

An analysis was undertaken of the relationship between average maternal commitment scores and each of the behavioral role expectations already discussed. The findings indicate that "undisguised" and "concern" were the two role expectations with highest maternal commitment, whereas mothers who saw control and formality as expectations had lower scores. This was the direction of the response only, however, and the differences were not statistically significant.

Mothers' motivation for role incumbency, or how ready they were to place their children and assume the role of "mother with child in foster care," was considered to be another variable relevant to mothers' behavioral expectations. The responses used to measure that dimension were those given by mothers in answering the following question: "Looking back at everything that has happened, would you say that the placement of your child was absolutely necessary, very necessary, somewhat necessary, or not necessary at all?" Each mother had only one choice. Forty-seven percent considered the placement to be "absolutely necessary," 17 percent said it was "very necessary," 13 percent "somewhat necessary," and 23 percent said placement was "not necessary at all."

Those replies were scaled from 1 to 4, with 1 representing the most negative answer, "not at all necessary" (considered to be low maternal motivation for placement) and 4 representing the most positive answer of "absolutely necessary" (high maternal motivation for placement). When these scores were related to behavioral role expectations, it was found that women noting "acquiescent" as a role expectation were significantly less motivated to place children in care than others. This finding is of interest, since it implies that the seeming acquiescence is not related to a basic willingness to accept place-ment, but rather to objections to placement and a resistance to role in-cumbency.

Expectations attached to any particular role can be influenced by one's evaluation of the performances of the institution to which the role is attached. Thus the final set of variables analyzed related to the mothers' estimates of how well the foster care system was functioning. A four-part index was constructed that included respondents' replies on the effects of placement upon the child, their general feelings about foster care, and their attitudes toward placement agencies on two di-mensions specifically defined—whether they saw agencies as facilita-tors of child care, or as usurpers of parental rights.[16]

The question, "In your opinion has foster care had any effect on your child?" with an accompanying probe for affirmative answers to determine the nature of the effect, was posed in the study interview. Twenty-four percent said there was a positive effect, giving such re-plies as, "He seems fat and happy"; 34 percent saw a negative effect, such things as, "He's very nervous now," or "He has become so withdrawn"; 35 percent of mothers said placement had had no effect on their child; and the remaining 7 percent did not answer.

A second evaluation question utilized was, "Thinking back over the entire period of time that your child has been in placement, would you share with us your feelings about foster care placement?" Thirty-nine percent of mothers gave positive responses, saying such things as "wonderful," "good," "best thing for the child." An al-most equal number, 37 percent, responded negatively, saying they had "rotten" feelings about the placement, were "very upset" about it, or "didn't like it at all." A smaller group, 22 percent, were ambivalent, reporting both good and bad feelings about foster care and making such statements as "the children miss me but they seem happy," or "I

[16] The "surrogate" dimension of agency attitudes, defined in chapter 1, was not used in the analysis of role expectations, since it represented a nonevaluative position.

feel unhappy about it but I know it's good for the children." A few remaining mothers, 2 percent, did not answer.[17]

Mothers' attitudes toward agencies have been a key variable throughout the study analysis. Two categories were utilized with reference to behavioral role expectations: the agency as a facilitator of child care and the agency as a usurper of parental rights. Scores of mothers in response to each of these attitudes were calculated and included in the evaluation index. These scores, combined with scores reflecting mothers' feelings about placement and estimate of the effect of placement on the child, all computed on a continuum from negative to positive, comprised the evaluation index. With a possible range of 4 to 12, the average evaluation score for mothers was 8.8. Correlations of each variable with the index were again computed, and they ranged from .55 to .69.

Mothers who felt they should be "controlled" when with the caseworker evaluated placement significantly more negatively than did women who did not indicate that behavior as expected. Similarly, a more negative evaluation was found for women noting "acquiescent" as an expectation, although this was not statistically significant.

Summary

Mothers with children in care vary widely in what they perceive to be appropriate role expectations in relation to agency caseworkers. The five major kinds of behavior suggested were control, formality, acquiescence, to be undisguised, and to express concern for the child. Al-

---

[17] Data concerning feelings about placement reported in this chapter are based on responses of 128 mothers interviewed at time II in 1968, whose children were still in care. Evaluation data reported in chapter 4 are based on 186 time III interviews in 1971, and include responses from both mothers with children in care and mothers whose children had been discharged. More positive feelings were expressed about placement at time III than in the interim interview.

though behavior in more than one of these categories was mentioned by most of the mothers, there was enough concentration of expectations to enable a number of analyses to be made relating role expectations to relevant study variables.

"Undisguised" as a role expectation was most likely to be mentioned by white mothers, by those in the study's highest socioeconomic circumstances, by women with children in agencies administered under Jewish auspices, in small-sized agencies, and in residential treatment centers, and by mothers who talked about themselves with the agency caseworkers and were highly motivated for role incumbency. "Controlled" as a role expectation was most likely to be mentioned by Black women, by mothers in the lowest socioeconomic circumstances, by women with children in foster home care and in Protestant agencies, by women who talked about discharge and visiting but had relatively few contacts with the agency caseworker, and by mothers who had a relatively low maternal commitment according to the criteria used and a negative evaluation of placement. Those mothers who stressed "to display concern for the child" as an appropriate role expectation were most frequently either Black or Puerto Rican, of middle or low socioeconomic circumstances, with children in large-sized agencies, women who talked about how their children were getting along in placement but had infrequent contacts with agency workers, and who had a high degree of maternal commitment and a relatively positive evaluation of placement.

The role expectation "to be formal," was most frequently mentioned by Puerto Rican mothers, by mothers in low or middle socioeconomic circumstances, by women whose children were placed in agencies under Catholic auspices, by mothers with relatively low maternal commitment on the index and a high motivation for role incumbency, feeling placement to be very necessary. "Acquiescent" as a role expectation was significantly related to only one of the variables tested, low motivation for role incumbency, but tended to be stronger for mothers having a child in an agency administered under nonsectarian auspices, for mothers who talked with the agency caseworker about discharge or visiting of the child, for black mothers, and for those having a negative evaluation of placement.

There are implications in these findings for both practice and further research. The worker needs to be aware of the range of behavioral expectations held by clients, and to differentiate between overt behavior and underlying feelings of mothers. The worker also needs to question and evaluate the extent to which agency and professionals are in fact defining how mothers are supposed to behave. One research inquiry that would be of interest would be directed to studying workers' behavioral expectations, e.g., how do they think they should behave in relation to clients with specified problem backgrounds? The issue of congruence of expectations as between worker and client could be examined. Furthermore, the differentiation found among expectations of mothers could be compared with the range of worker expectations.

Seven

Family Forms and Household Composition

A serendipitous reward of a longitudinal study is the opportunity, over time, to reexamine basic assumptions and rethink study concepts. This research began with the intent of exploring experiences, problems, and reactions of the biological families of children in foster care. It was not until after the first field interview was completed in 1966, and the data were examined, that the complications of describing family composition itself were apparent. In the second interview, late in 1968, an effort was made to derive data on family functioning. Only about half the children were still in care at that time, however, so that the potential sample was severely limited. Furthermore, even for the discharged children, a valid index of family functioning could not be developed from data gathered in a single interview in which this matter comprised only one small segment of the interview content. Much more intensive work, and data from a variety of sources, would be needed before scores on family functioning could be validated.[1]

In the third field interview, the study focused on household composition and family forms. Two basic questions were asked: "What does family mean to you?" and "Who is in your family?" The answers to these give some new insights into the life-styles and patterns of living of the families in the sample studied, as well as the mothers' perceptions of their own relationships—perceptions that were often nontraditional.

The substantial literature on the family as an institution has stressed its pervasive, universal, and functional aspects. There are several dimensions to an examination of family structure that will be used in the analysis of the study sample. Two elements often included in the concept of family are the idea of "family of orientation" and that of "family of procreation." The former refers to the family into which an individual is born, including his or her own mother, father, siblings, aunts, uncles, and grandparents. The latter refers to the family that the adult individual creates, including his or her spouse, children, and grandchildren. A further distinction in family forms is made between the nuclear and the extended family. Nuclear family usually refers to husband and wife and their own natural or adopted children. Extended family usually refers to persons related by blood or kinship to members of the nuclear family. When the members are living together, the former is generally termed the nuclear family household and the latter the extended family household. Three other household types or constellations should be noted. These are husband and wife

---

[1] The agency phase of the child welfare study, although not operationalizing the concept of "functioning," did ask workers for a global assessment of whether or not families had improved from the date of initial placement to the first worker interview, a period of six to eight months. Improvement was defined as "any form of visible change for the better described by the workers." This included attitudinal change as well as environmental improvement. The report of the agency study indicates that family situations were judged to be unimproved in 60 percent of the cases and improved in 40 percent. See Deborah Shapiro, "Agency Investment in Foster Care: A Study," *Social Work,* 17, No. 4 (July 1972), 22.

living together without children, either because they have none or because their adult children have their own households; the single-parent household comprising an adult and his or her children; and the single adult living alone or with unrelated persons.

Discussions of family as an institution are often concerned with the social functions performed. Among these are the following: (1) reproduction, (2) economic sharing and cooperation, (3) institutionalization of social fatherhood, (4) establishment through marriage of alliances outside of blood relationships, (5) bestowing social identity on members (status placement), (6) nurture and primary socialization of the child, and (7) stabilization of the adult personality (emotional maintenance).[2]

Not every family in any society performs all of these functions. Although most families follow a typical style, there is always a part of every population that is organized in atypical family forms, which are therefore structured in such a way that they perform fewer than all the family functions noted above. The one-parent family formed with the birth of an out-of-wedlock child, for example, does not function to institutionalize social fatherhood, nor does it establish through marriage alliances outside of blood relationships. The one-parent family formed through the death of a spouse, however, continues to maintain these functions. Childless couples do not perform the reproductive function. One pertinent example is that of biological families with children in foster care placement who have, at least temporarily, relegated the responsibility for nurture and primary socialization of their children to social agencies.

As Stack and Semmel point out, the nuclear family is not the only unit of domestic cooperation. The study they report on, dealing with poor Black families in a midwestern city, supports other evidence to the effect that the universal functions of family life can be and are

---

[2] William J. Goode, *Readings on the Family and Society* (Englewood Cliffs, N.J.: Prentice-Hall, 1964); Rose Coser, ed., *The Family: Its Structure and Function* (New York: St. Martins Press, 1964); Talcott Parsons and Robert F. Bales, *Family, Socialization and Interaction Process* (Glencoe, Ill.: The Free Press, 1955).

provided by other social units.[3] They go on to say, "Where people sleep does not reveal the scope of the domestic network which may be diffused over several kin-based households." [4] To understand the life-styles of the study sample, therefore, it is necessary to know about both household composition and family definitions and forms.

For the country as a whole, in spite of the traditional prototype, census data indicate that in 1972, at approximately the time the final data for the present study were being collected, the nuclear family comprising husband, wife, and children under 18 years made up only 48 percent of all United States families. Husband-wife pairs without children under 18 made up 38 percent of all families. The remaining units comprised 14 percent of the total and were almost entirely female-headed households, only half of which contained children.[5] The characteristics of New York City families at that time differed in one main respect from the total United States. Whereas 48 percent of United States families included husband, wife, and dependent children, only 38 percent of New York City families were made up of that basic nuclear-family unit. Husband-wife units with no children made up 41 percent of the New York City total. The remaining 21 percent of families in New York City were mostly female-headed households, half with children and half without.[6]

The demographic analysis of the study sample clearly shows that what may be deviant for the population at large was typical for

[3] U.S. Congress, Subcommittee on Fiscal Policy of the Joint Economic Committee, *The Concept of Family in the Poor Black Community*, by Carol B. Stack and Herbert Semmel, Studies in Public Welfare, Paper No. 12 (Part II) (Washington, D.C., 1973), p. 275.

[4] Ibid., p. 276.

[5] U.S. Bureau of the Census, "Household and Family Characteristics: March, 1972," *Current Population Reports, Population Characteristics*, Series P-20, No. 246 (Washington, D.C., 1972), table 1.

[6] Barbara D. Hanrieder and Raymond A. Glazier, *Characteristics of the Population in New York City Health Areas: 1970, No. 3: Family Composition*, Department of Research and Program Planning Information (New York: Community Council of Greater New York, Inc., October 1973).

these families. Just before placement, for example, only 15 percent of study children in the follow-up sample of 160 families were living with two biological parents who were married to each other. At the time of the third study interview, more than half of the women (56 percent) were the only adult members of their households. Just over one quarter (27 percent), were living with husbands.[7] Ten percent were living with relatives (own mothers, own fathers, aunts and/or uncles) and 6 percent with friends. The household composition of 2 of the women was not ascertainable. Four out of five of the sample families (82 percent) had at least one child present in their home. The constellation of adults in the home had little relationship to whether or not a child was also present.

Other variables were related to the household composition of the study group. Puerto Rican women were more likely to be living without other adults in the household (65 percent) than were either Black women (55 percent) or white women (41 percent). White women in the sample were more likely to be living with their husbands (50 percent) than were Black and Puerto Rican mothers (20 percent for each). The lower the socioeconomic status of the mothers, the more likely they were to be living without other adults, this being the case for 25 percent of women in the highest socioeconomic group, 66 percent of the middle group, and 70 percent of the mothers in the lowest socioeconomic group. Age was also a factor, with 80 percent of study mothers who lived with adult relatives being under thirty years old. Finally, as would be expected, marital status and household composition were related, with 72 percent of the married women living with husbands. Women who were divorced, separated, widowed, or had never married were most likely to be living without other adults.

The most striking finding to emerge from the data on household composition is that the majority of the mothers in the study, at the time of the third interview five years after placement, were follow-

[7] In only two of those cases was there another adult in the household as well. In both cases that other adult was a distant relative of the study mother.

ing neither the typical American pattern of living with nuclear con-
jugal family nor the expected alternative of living with an extended
family. Instead, 56 percent of the study mothers were living as single-
parent families and functioning as household heads.

Definitions of Family

The concept of family is much broader and more meaningful than that
of household. It is also harder to define. To avoid imposing a precon-
ceived notion on the respondents, an open question was asked of the
mother and the spontaneous answers were recorded. The question was,
"The word 'family' means different things to different people. We'd
like to get your definition. What does the word 'family' mean to
you?"

Mothers interpreted the question in different ways, as was apparent from the groupings of answers. Twenty-five percent responded
by reference to the family as a constellation of persons. Answers included statements such as "family means mother, father, and child,"
or "mother and child." About three-fourths of these references were
to the family of procreation only, and one-fourth to both the family of
procreation and that of orientation, including extended family. One
Puerto Rican respondent, for example, said, "Family is brothers, sis-
ters, nephews, nieces, cousins, father, mother, children, grandparents,
and great-grandparents."

About two-thirds of all mothers responded to the question on
the meaning of family in terms of positive attitudes, feelings, or emo-
tions. These answers fell into several categories, which overlapped to
some extent, but each of which had a main theme. The number of
mothers responding in each category is noted below (some mothers
giving multiple answers).

1. *Family means togetherness, a unity of significant persons*
(56 mothers). Examples are, "All of us being together"; "A group

that's together"; "I believe family is all the persons that live together." These responses included physical proximity, or living together, as well as a sense of unity and belonging. Form was also important. One mother said, "A family should be together on holidays, Father's Day, Mother's Day, and go out together on Sunday."

2. *Family means closeness, caring, being concerned, loving* (34 mothers). Examples are, "People who care for each other"; "People who are close to each other"; "Beloved ones."

3. *Family means sharing, cooperation, helping each other* (21 mothers). Examples are, "Share things together"; "Help each other out." One mother said, "Family is people you can turn to for help when you are in trouble." Another said, "If you are sick they will be there."

4. *Family means happiness* (8 mothers). Examples were, "It means to be happy," or "What makes you feel good."

5. *Family means understanding or being understood* (6 mothers). Examples are, "You can go to them and they will understand you"; "To understand one another."

In terms of the various functions of the family, as discussed in the literature and cited earlier in this chapter, these data indicate that the majority of mothers spontaneously define family in terms of its function of maintenance and stabilization of the adult personality. The women who said family meant "closeness," "understanding," "sharing," "togetherness," or "happiness" were all stressing the personal and emotional stabilization aspects of that social institution.

Only 2 mothers introduced some other traditional family functions in their definitions. One said, "Family was a way to raise children decently—to teach them right from wrong." A second mother said, "To me, family means security."

For the remaining 12 mothers, or 7 percent of respondents, "family" meant neither a constellation of persons nor a positive feeling, but either an absence of reaction or a strong negative emotion. Six mothers said the concept of family meant nothing to them. One said,

"I don't know what you mean—I have no family to speak of. I don't know my mother or father. I was raised by friends." Another said, "I never had a family. I don't know." A third mother said, "Family means nothing to me. I don't know what family is. I never had a real family."

For the remaining 6 mothers, the question brought forth bitter, negative emotional responses. One mother said, "Family is for the birds—everyone is out for themselves." Another said, "I hate the word 'family.' It makes me remember how bitter I am about my parents and my sister." A third mother said, "My mother, father, and sister are no special part of my life—they couldn't care less about me or my children." Finally, one mother said, "Family to me means total confusion and hate."

In spite of these few negative reactions, the evidence strongly suggests the concept of family was positive and meaningful to these mothers. Basically, as a group, they stressed three aspects: togetherness, caring, and sharing. Factors such as the mothers' socioeconomic status, age, and to a limited extent, ethnic group, birthplace, and marital status were related to which concepts were stressed. Women of the lowest socioeconomic status were twice as likely to mention the constellation of persons included in the family than were others. Mothers in the highest socioeconomic group were twice as likely to mention "togetherness" in their family definitions. "Understanding" was most likely to be a "high status" response and "happiness" a "low status" reply. No differences existed for "sharing" or "caring" responses on this socioeconomic variable.

"Sharing" and "caring" as definitions were, however, related to the age of the mother. The younger a woman was, the more likely she was to convey the idea of "sharing" as she spontaneously defined family. "Caring" was mentioned by the youngest and the oldest mothers, but not by those in the middle group. Finally, married women were significantly more likely to include the concept of "togetherness" in their definition of family than were the unmarried mothers.

Persons Included in Family

In order to move from generalizations to specific descriptive data, all respondents were asked, "When you speak of your own family, whom do you include?" Almost all of the respondents, 96 percent, mentioned their own children as members of their families. Only 62 percent of the women mentioned their own mothers (the placed child's grandmother) and 46 percent mentioned their own fathers (the placed child's grandfather). Siblings were mentioned by 66 percent of all respondents, and 23 percent mentioned other relatives as family members, mainly aunts and uncles. Fewer than one-third of all respondents, 32 percent, mentioned husbands as members of the family. Three percent of women included nonrelatives whom they regarded as family.

After each respondent spontaneously mentioned who was in the family, the interviewer, if certain relations were not mentioned, would inquire why they had been excluded. The probe might be, for example, "Is there any special reason you didn't mention your mother?" Death was a relevant factor: 12 percent of respondents did not mention their own mothers because the mothers were dead, and this was true for 45 percent who did not mention their own fathers; 4 percent had deceased husbands, and for 1 percent a sibling had died.

When living persons were not mentioned as family members, there were three main explanations: (1) lack of physical closeness, (2) lack of emotional closeness, and (3) outright hostility. The first would be illustrated by a response such as "He (or she) lives far away"; the second by, "We were never really close"; and the third by, "There is bad feeling between us." The most frequently noted reason for not mentioning their own mothers or their husbands was lack of emotional closeness. One mother said she didn't mention her separated husband as family because she "could never count on him for help." Another said she didn't mention her husband because "he doesn't love me." Omission of own father or siblings was mainly due to their living far away. A fourth explanation was given only for the omission of one's own father as a family member. One out of five women who did not mention their own father said, "I never knew him."

A higher percentage of Puerto Rican women, 74 percent, included their own mothers in their families than did either the Black or the white women, 53 percent and 59 percent respectively. This was true also of siblings: 83 percent of Puerto Rican women noted siblings as members of their family, as compared to 75 percent of white women and 45 percent of Black women. Husbands as part of their families were mentioned by 50 percent of white mothers, 30 percent of Blacks, and 23 percent of Puerto Ricans. Only 34 percent of Black women mentioned their own fathers, as compared with 55 percent of white mothers and 53 percent of Puerto Ricans.

With regard to socioeconomic status, about twice as many women in the highest group included husbands as members of their family than did others. With respect to age of the mother, the younger a woman was, the more likely she was to mention her own mother as a member of her family; 77 percent of the teen-agers did so, 63 percent of women in their twenties, 62 percent of the women in their thirties, and 50 percent of women forty years old or over.

Relationship to Child's Father

In securing data on family relationships, mothers were asked about their marital status. The interview instrument also included questions that explicitly obtained data on who was the mother and father for each child in the study. There was no attempt at verification, however, or checking out of licenses. If a mother said she was married, she was so recorded. Thus, long-standing consensual unions would probably be included in the married group.

According to the mothers' own reports, 61 percent of them had been married to the placed child's father at one time. Two-thirds of this group reported that they were still married to him, whereas one-third were divorced or widowed. Thus five years after the original placement, 40 percent of the study mothers stated they were still married to the father of their placed child.

Since only 15 percent of mothers in the follow-up sample were both married to and living with their children's father at the time of placement, and another 2 percent were living with but not married to the father, an important question that arises is whether or not the mother and/or child continued to have a relationship with the absent parent. Two questions were asked with appropriate probes: "Was the mother in touch with the father?" and "Did the child see the father?" The responses were that, in addition to the 17 percent of mothers who were living with the father of their placed child, 30 percent were in touch with him, seeing him, either regularly or sporadically. However, the majority of the study mothers, 53 percent, reported having no contact at all with their placed child's father.

In most cases, if the mother was living with or in contact with the father, so was her placed child. If the mother was not seeing the father, then typically neither was the child. In 9 cases, however, the child was reported by the mother as seeing the father, although the mother had no contact. And in 13 cases, the mother reported that she saw the father, whereas the child did not. In terms of ethnic differences, 60 percent of white mothers were in contact with their child's father; this was the case for 25 percent of Black and of Puerto Rican mothers. More contact was maintained by mothers in the highest socioeconomic group, 65 percent, than by those in the lowest or middle group, where in both cases only 39 percent were in touch with their children's fathers.

Household and Family— Relationships and Relatives

The data on households and families of mothers whose children have been placed in foster care point up some of the complications of relationships and relatives. The majority of these women, 56 percent, lived in single-parent households, only about one quarter were living with husbands, and the rest lived with relatives and friends. This did not mean, however, that they did not offer strong positive definitions for the word "family." In spite of the prevalence of single-parent households, the dominant concept expressed was "togetherness." Families, in theory, were looked on as providing emotional strength and supports—they are the people who help you when you are in trouble. The responses were idealized, however, since only about two-thirds of mothers reported close relatives such as mother, father, or siblings as being significant family members.

One important reason for examining the households of this sample was to see the extent to which they differed from the population at large. A review of national and local data shows that, although the sample is very different from the average or typical household, there has been a strong trend over the last few decades in the country as a whole in the direction of the living arrangements of families in this study.

An analysis of national data shows a substantial rise in the female-headed household, a rise that can be attributed not to a decline in husband-wife households, but to a decline in the share of "subfamilies" there are in the total. (One type of "subfamily" might be composed of a mother living with her children in a household headed by her father or uncle.) Lerman, in reviewing the data, states, "Among women living with their own children under 18 but not living with a husband, the share heading subfamilies fell from 33 percent in 1950 to 13 percent in 1972, with a corresponding rise in the share heading families from 67 percent to 87 percent." [8]

In further analysis of this phenomenon Cutright and Scanzoni show that the percentage of mothers aged 15–44 in disrupted mar-

[8] U.S. Congress, Subcommittee on Fiscal Policy of the Joint Economic Committee, *The Family, Poverty, and Welfare Programs: An Introductory Essay on Problems of Analysis and Policy,* by Robert I. Lerman, Studies in Public Welfare, Paper No. 12 (Part I) (Washington, D.C., 1973), p. 275.

riages (separated, widowed, or divorced) who were family heads increased from 43 to 79 percent between 1940 and 1970. They go on to say that this change in the propensity to form separate households (rather than living as a child or other relative of the family head) is similar to shifts toward separate housing and living arrangements among younger married couples, aged couples, and widowed persons.[9]

A number of factors help to explain this growth in single-parent, female-headed households, and it is difficult to separate them out to show the strength of each influence. Among the factors is the nature of assistance programs and the entitlements of recipients; the relative availability of housing for large and small family units; and the changing social mores. The women's movement, in particular, has helped minimize the stigma generally placed on the female-headed household and has given moral support to women who choose to function as family heads, as well as to women who find themselves in that role, regardless of choice. Thus although the study sample is still atypical for the general population, the trend is in the direction of convergence. These trends have implications for mothers with children formerly in care who are heads of single-parent households. As the issues affecting the single parent secure more national attention, they are more likely to be subject to universal, rather than selective, social policies. Supports for the single-parent family can help prevent foster care, as well as helping to reestablish the family unit if placement has occurred.

The strong interest expressed by the study mothers in the meaning of "family," and the prevalence of the sharing, caring, togetherness definitions, imply that the family was a meaningful institution for respondents. The principal family functions, however, are not seen as the traditional ones of economic support and certifying legitimacy of children. Emotional supports, closeness, people who are there in time of trouble—these are the more humanist definitions of

[9] Idem., *Income Supplements and the American Family,* by Phillips Cutright and John Scanzoni, Studies in Public Welfare, Paper No. 12 (Part I), p. 55.

family expressed by mothers with children in care, mothers who are primarily poor and Black and Puerto Rican. The mode of analysis that postulates the decline of the minority family may be due in part to a simplistic analysis of the data, which confuses household composition with family. The social forces that produce the single-parent, female-headed household do not thereby destroy the family. The family takes different forms and its functions are met in both new and old ways. To analyze changes in household composition as synonymous with changes in family is to undermine the latter institution and identify as weakness what in fact may be strength.

Eight

No-fault Foster Care: A Summary Proposal

The longitudinal study has provided answers to the questions raised, "What happens to families when children are in placement?" and "What chronic needs persist after the crisis passes?" The data also provide an evaluation of the foster care system from the point of view of the clients. The final chapter will summarize the circumstances of these families, show how there may be a differential experience with services depending on reason for placement, and suggest implications for practice and the need for "no-fault" foster care.

Families Five Years after Placement

Five years after children entered care, 73 percent had been discharged, primarily to their own homes. The majority of mothers had thus renewed their child-caring role and stabilized their home situations. The crisis resulting in foster care had passed for most children, but the chronic conditions that underlay their placement still persisted. Most families were living on the borderline of self-management, in terms of income, health, and stability of relationships.

Financially, the situations of mothers appear to have somewhat worsened over the five years. At the time of placement 45 percent of the follow-up sample of 160 mothers were receiving public assistance as their main support, and an additional 3 percent as supplementary support. This group, together with those with incomes of less than $75 a week, comprised approximately 60 percent of all mothers who could be considered to be living at or below the poverty level. Five years later, the percentage of these mothers on public assistance had risen to 58 percent for full-time support, plus 13 percent for supplementary support. The total percentage with incomes below the poverty level had risen to over 70 percent of the sample. The rise in public assistance cases is partly accounted for by the decline, over the five-year period, in numbers of mothers who were institutionalized, hospitalized for mental or physical illness, or in jail. Although those mothers had not been receiving public assistance, they were in fact public charges. When they were able to maintain themselves in the community, the source of their support shifted from other budgets to the public assistance rolls.

For the total group, there was little movement toward self-support over the five-year period. There were only 10 mothers who had received public assistance at the time of placement but were working and self-supporting five years later. In 9 of these cases, however, the children were still in foster care, which represents another kind of subsidy. Although the numbers were small, this finding does raise the question of whether an appropriate success criterion for any one social service can be determined without considering total family needs. If going to work and getting off welfare means that children have to be maintained in long-term foster care, this implies that the goals of the public welfare system may be at variance with the goals of its own child welfare programs, which presumably seek the return of children

to their own homes. In fact the much maligned AFDC support probably is the most successful preventive program for keeping children out
of foster care. The findings speak to the need for integration of services and consistency of goals.

The residential movement of families over the five-year period
was substantially higher than that of the total population. Eighty-one
percent of the 160 mothers were living at different addresses by the
time of the third interview. In terms of neighborhood, according to the
criteria used, conditions improved for 28 percent of families,
worsened for 15 percent, and remained the same for the remaining 57
percent. When the direction of movement is examined, 24 percent
moved to another address in the same neighborhood, 27 percent to
another neighborhood in the same borough, and 23 percent to another
borough. Of this last group the moves were mainly from Manhattan to
Brooklyn and the Bronx.

Although there were many changes of relationships over the
five-year period, over two-thirds of the mothers were in the same marital status as at the beginning of the study. Five years after placement
the majority of mothers, 56 percent, lived in single-parent female-
headed households, 27 percent lived with their husbands, 10 percent
with relatives, and 6 percent with friends. Establishment of own
household was an important phenomenon, and this followed the national trend of subfamilies moving out from extended family households and establishing independent units.

In discussing placement and the foster care system, mothers
were able to express feelings and relate experiences. Feelings on
placement tended to diminish in intensity over the years. Bitterness
dropped sharply, and there was a decline of sadness, worry, and nervousness and a rise in relief and thankfulness. The feelings that persisted most strongly over the years were guilt, anger, and shame. By
the end of the study there were discernible shifts in feeling referents,
with mothers showing more ability to relate to the child and the child's
needs and less self-involvement.

In evaluating foster care, approximately half the mothers in the

final field interview expressed positive, satisfied feelings about placement, about one-fourth were negative and disapproving, and the remaining one-fourth were ambivalent or neutral. Since there is no comparative yardstick for client evaluation of services, it is impossible to
evaluate these data in terms of relative success. Even though the majority of mothers expressed satisfaction with the child care received,
most of them felt placement to be a last alternative, and few would
recommend it to other mothers in need of help. The most positive reactions to placement were from families who were in the highest socioeconomic circumstances in the study sample. In addition, those
mothers perceived workers as being more helpful, interested, understanding, and better in communicating than did other mothers.

When mothers looked at the broader picture of social services,
they reported most favorably on individualized help and personalized
contacts with workers. Agencies most frequently used were the Department of Social Services for income maintenance, and hospitals and
mental health clinics for illness. Use of other services was lower than
expected, and in particular Black mothers made significantly less use
of all services except income and health than did either whites or
Puerto Ricans. Mothers in the highest socioeconomic circumstances in
the study tended to use more community services and perceive them as
more helpful than did others. Approximately two-thirds of all mothers
perceived self-help as the most important factor in improving their situations. The heavy use of welfare, hospitals, and clinics shows the interrelationship of income, health, and child welfare needs. Mothers
saw money and health as their main problems at the time of placement, but when asked about primary prevention, most mothers referred to interpersonal factors and early childhood difficulties in their
own families.

The study explored two new areas, role expectations of
mothers as clients and family forms and definitions. These findings led
to some new insights into how mothers perceive their situations. In the
first instance, it was found that mothers had very definite ideas as to
how they were supposed to behave in relation to workers. The major

categories into which these perceptions fell included "to be undisguised," "to be controlled," and "to be acquiescent," and these
expectations were significantly related to a number of study variables,
including ethnicity. The practice implications here are obvious—
workers need to know role expectations of clients in order to interpret
their behavior appropriately.

The investigation of family definitions and family members, in
relation to household composition, also provides findings important to
practice. The majority of women lived in single-parent, female-headed
households, but they defined "family" primarily in terms of "togetherness," "sharing," and "caring." The implication drawn is that
family concepts and household composition are two very different
phenomena. The prevalence of the single-parent household, made up
of mother and children, does not necessarily mean the absence of family constellations. Different family forms are emerging in response to
economic and social pressures, but new strengths may be found in
kinship groups who may live separately but have strong familial ties.

Socially Approved and Socially Unacceptable Reasons for Placement

Early in the study, when baseline data were being analyzed, it was apparent that the reason for placement was a critical factor that related
significantly to many other study variables. As the study proceeded
through two additional field interviews, a new pattern began to
emerge. Certain placement reasons tended to group together, and relate in consistent ways to parental attitudes and experiences. The underlying dimensions found concerned whether the reason for placement tended to be more acceptable or less in terms of broad social and
legal norms of behavior. For example, it is acceptable to be sick, but
not to be an addict. It is acceptable to have a disturbed child, but not
to abandon it. The reasons that grouped together empirically and were
labeled "socially approved" were the following: physical illness,

mental illness, emotional disturbance of the child, and unwillingness or inability of the mother of the infant born out of wedlock to assume care. On the other hand, four quite different reasons also grouped together and these were labeled "socially unacceptable." These were abandonment, severe neglect and abuse, severe family dysfunction including addiction, alcoholism, retardation and incarceration, and unwillingness or inability of the child-caring person to continue care. When these two categories were used, data fell into place and numerous significant differences emerged.

Some examples of differences between the two groups of mothers in feelings, attitudes, and opinions are cited in table 6 to show the importance of this analysis.

Table 6. Selected Significant Differences in Maternal Responses by Placement Groupings

Socially Approved		Socially Unacceptable
Thankful feelings at placement	(1)	Angry feelings at placement
Positive evaluation of foster care	(2)	Negative evaluation of foster care
Higher rating of worker interest, understanding, helpfulness, communication	(3)	Lower rating of worker interest, understanding, helpfulness, communication
Fewer problems in visiting	(4)	More problems in visiting
70 percent use community services	(5)	30 percent use community services
71 percent find "others" helpful	(6)	29 percent find "others" helpful
77 percent found placement agencies helpful	(7)	46 percent found placement agencies helpful

These differences are probably due to several factors, all of which bear further investigation. The first and most obvious explanation is that the mothers in the "unacceptable" category are a more pathological group, harder to reach, resistant to services, and with more difficult problems. The differential factor, however, is not the severity of the problem but the accessibility to services. The mother dying of cancer, or with severe mental illness, has problems that may be more serious in terms of life experience than the neglectful or abusive mother, but she is more likely to be a supporter of the placement system than the mother who rejects the social norms.

A second factor contributing to poor client perceptions of the system may be the workers' attitudes to clients, and their acceptance or rejection of families in need of services. Problems of working with hard-to-reach clients have been well documented. In the course of this study, when these data were reported to a group of child welfare workers at a professional conference and reactions sought, one worker responded as follows, "But surely you don't expect us to like mothers who beat their children." Another participant in that session whose job included taking children to foster homes for placement said "The first question foster mothers ask is 'why was he placed?' If the reason was the mother has tuberculosis, for example, the foster mother will say 'Poor thing, tell her I will take good care of him. Tell her not to worry.' If the reason is drugs or child beating, the response often is 'Keep that mother away from this house and away from the child.' "

There are many kinds of problems that arise in dealing with unmotivated, resistant clients. Billingsley, for example, studied role deprivation of workers in family agencies as compared with those in child protective services. Role deprivation was conceptualized as the discrepancy between how workers allocate their time and how they would prefer to allocate it. His findings showed that role deprivation was shown by 77 percent of workers in the child protective agency studied, but by only 26 percent of their counterparts in the family agency, a highly significant difference.[1]

The problems faced by child care workers are formidable, especially when dealing with severe family pathology. Yet the field depends heavily on relatively youthful and untrained workers, and the turnover rate is substantial. Shapiro analyzed the backgrounds of 1,200 child welfare workers who worked with the 624 children in the

[1] Andrew Billingsley, *The Role of the Social Worker in a Child Protective Agency: A Comparative Analysis,* unpublished doctoral dissertation (Waltham, Mass.: Brandeis University, 1964).

original Child Welfare Study sample. She found that 69 percent were under the age of thirty, 78 percent had just the B.A. degree and only 22 percent the M.S. degree. The median total years of experience of the 1,200 workers averaged two years.[2] The turnover rate for child welfare workers was measured by Shapiro in a subsample of 220 cases. Over the four-year period from 1966–70, only 19 percent of the workers were in the same agency with the same position, 36 percent were in the same agency but a different position and presumably relating to different children, and 55 percent, the majority, either were working in another agency, were working in an occupation other than social work, or were out of the labor market.[3]

A third approach to explaining the differences between those who had "approved" and those who had "unacceptable" reasons for placement refers to neither client nor worker but to the foster care system, which may in fact provide differential services for different kinds of clients. Children who enter residential treatment centers, for example, are likely to receive therapy as well as family services. Neglected children in the congregate institutions will not be likely to receive specialized services, even though clinically they may be indistinguishable from the "disturbed" group. Thus how the child enters the system, rather than his or her needs and the parents' problems, can result in differential services. This means that mothers' perceptions may be more than an artifact of their own pathology or worker reactions. They may instead reflect the actual services given.

A final issue that the study findings suggest is the place in the foster care system accorded to biological parents. This is not a phenomenon of this sample alone. In an extensive British study of foster care George concludes that one of the "fundamental issues" in foster care is the part natural parents should play in the lives of their placed

[2] Deborah Shapiro, *Agencies and Children: A Child Welfare Network's Investment in its Clients* (New York: Columbia University Press, forthcoming), chapter 2.

[3] Deborah Shapiro, "Occupational Mobility and Child Welfare Workers: An Exploratory Study," *Child Welfare*, 43, No. 1 (January 1974), p. 8.

children. He notes that the problems and demands of parenthood have been complicated in industrial societies. He states, however, that

society stigmatizes those parents who do not fulfil their role adequately, with the result that legislation and social institutions and services adopt a semi-punitive, condescending attitude towards such parents. The parents' failure to fulfil their role is attributed to personal, psychological or moral inadequacies rather than to cultural, social and economic factors which are institutional in contemporary societies. It is in effect a similar view to the nineteenth-century belief that unemployment was a moral failure of the individual worker and not the result of the economic system. We have today acknowledged the concept of structural unemployment that affects workers in a way that is largely beyond their ability to counter. We need to accept the truth of the same process being at work in the case of parental failure in child upbringing. The change that is long overdue is not to reduce the parenting role content but to provide the services which are necessary for the adequate implementation of the parenting role.[4]

Specifically, George outlines the need for the universal supporting services, such as employment, housing, and family counseling, as a foundation for the meaningful provision of the substitute services, such as foster care. He goes on to point out one of the vicious circles engendered by the system, that the "active hostility or passive inaction towards natural parents" forces or allows them to alienate themselves from their children. This alienation then, in turn, is used as evidence against the parents and proof of their disinterest. In addition to stressing the primary effect of the structural faults in society rather than individual inadequacy as the basis for parental failure, George suggests recognition of another basic concept for child welfare, "that the needs and interests of parents and their children are interrelated and complementary rather than conflicting. . . ."[5]

The British study drew attention to the social stigma placed on

[4] V. George, *Foster Care, Theory and Practice* (London: Routledge and Kegan Paul, 1970), p. 219.

[5] Ibid., p. 220.

parents who fail to fulfill expected child-caring roles. The research reported in this volume shows that mothers perceive foster care dif-
ferently according to whether placement occurred because of socially
approved or socially unacceptable reasons. Both phenomena, the social stigma and the findings regarding differentiation in client perceptions, suggest the need for a "no-fault" foster care system.

The concept "no-fault" is introduced in a social rather than a
legal sense. It appears relevant when three conditions exist: when a
phenomenon is widely prevalent because of social forces beyond individual control; in a situation where assessment of blame is likely to be
dysfunctional; and for a condition where social benefits can ensue
from an appropriate sharing of risks. All three conditions apply to the
problems of child placement. Why children come into care is an important part of their social history needed for determination of individualized services, but not a criterion for provision of qualitatively different services.

The relevance of the research findings for the practice of child
welfare is implicit in much of the material that has been presented.
Some further explication, however, may be useful. The research supports a practice approach that (1) is family rather than child focused,
(2) seeks to minimize stigma, and (3) recognizes the economic and
social pressures placed on the institution of the family in present-day
society. Further integration is needed of the family and the child welfare service delivery systems, since both policies and practice may
become distorted when agency goals are identified with only one or
the other. A negative approach on the part of agencies toward biological families can serve as a self-fulfilling prophecy, thereby furthering
the alienation of parent and child.

The study finding indicating a shift in feeling referents in the
follow-up interview five years after placement has significance for
casework with biological mothers. The shift is from "self" as the
primary maternal feeling referent at the time of placement to "child"
five years later. This suggests a sequence in casework services for the
mother, in that the crisis must be handled first before the mother can

be expected to resume her accustomed role. Maternal concerns may be diminished at the point of personal difficulties, but this does not mean that they do not peak again when a better level of physical and mental health for the mother is attained.

The social work profession needs to cope with the finding that clients in better circumstances, with more strengths, make better use of help. Does this mean that more intensive work is needed for people with more severe problems, or does it mean that "quantity changes quality" and new directions and different service modalities are needed when multiple problems and client resistance are met? If this issue is not faced, the field will continue to give more to those who need less, and less to those who need more. The question may be raised as to whether scarce social work resources should not be put where the prospect of success is greatest. In practice, however, this has meant widening the gap between function and dysfunction, and allowing a pile-up of population groupings with severe deprivation. One further consequence is seen in client perception of services, e.g., the more problematic the situation, the less helpful are services perceived to be by the clients.

The new research findings on role expectations on the part of mothers in relation to caseworkers can have immediate application in casework practice. As part of their training workers need to know the nature of client preconceptions about what their own behavior with workers should be, and how these role expections can affect the casework interview. Client responses to the worker can only be interpreted appropriately in terms of the role expectations clients are seeking to fulfill.

When mothers were asked where their major source of help came from, the single most common answer was "myself." This was true regardless of services offered. This finding should be noted by caseworkers, since apparently the sense of self-help is what has most significance for these clients.

The research excursion into concepts of "family" suggests a different approach to family supports for this population. The growth in single-parent households should not be interpreted as implying a decline in family feeling. It may be that, in part, the independent household is an artifact of both the public assistance system and the available housing. The typical mother in the study reported broader family ties than just household members, and there is need to explore what strengths can be derived from these family relationships. Family concerns should not be described only in terms of monetary support or substitute child care—other family members often have burdens similar to those of the client. The practice field needs to explore how extended family members can be a source of support to clients in ways that are reasonable for their own situations.

Practitioners need to reexamine the role of biological parents, with emphasis on strengths and capacities rather than pathology and deficits. If the ideology of the practitioner conceives the foster care system as a social utility, a facilitator of child care when parents are unable to carry on, and recognizes the structural problems modern society imposes on the family system, then practice can offer more than lip service to "services to families." In those cases where the best professional judgment decides against reunion with biological families, then a satisfactory substitute long-term situation must be arranged for the child. In the majority of cases, however, the best interests of the child and the best interests of his own biological family are complementary rather than conflicting. A therapeutic approach rejects a stance that is based on workers' judgment of clients, assignment of guilt, or placement of stigma, on the theoretical basis that such an atmosphere does not provide for resolution of clients' problems. Yet in the field of child welfare the existence of a stigma on parents who place children has been widely described. In order to be helpful, services to such parents need to be free of judgment and not reinforce guilt. Practitioners need to examine their own feelings in working with natural parents, so that help can truly be offered.

The challenge to the foster care system is to put major efforts where the needs are greatest, rather than primarily where the prospects of success are the best. No-fault implies social sharing of costs, and elimination of the dysfunctional approach of stressing blame for inadequate parenting. The foster care system, rather than representing a philosophical alternative to own family care, should be a social utility available for those in need of services. In this latter role it can both meet the needs of children and share the risks undertaken by the poor in the assumption of parenthood.

Index

114; caseworker and, 98–101, 105–8, 113–15; demographic factors and, 107–8, 114–15; evaluation of placement and, 112–13, 114–15; maternal commitment and, 111, 114; necessity of placement and, 111–12, 114; practice implications of, 95, 111–12, 113–15, 135, 141

Role incumbency, see Necessity of placement

Salary, see Income, Support, main source of

Sauber, Mignon, 13n, 85n

Scanzoni, John, 128–29, 129n

School of child, contact with, 81, 82T, 84

Self as helpful factor, 76–77, 80, 93, 134, 141

Semmel, Herbert, 119–20, 120n

Sex of child, 48, 60

Shapiro, Deborah, 3n, 108n, 118n, 137–38, 138n

Shinn, Eugene B., 3n

Social attitudes, see Attitudes of parents, social

Social services, use of, 81–87, 93, 134; see also Community resources

Socially acceptable or disapproved reasons for placement, 14–15, 135–38, 136T; caseworker and, 64, 65, 72–73, 136T; community resources and, 93, 136T; evaluation of placement and, 59, 72–73, 81, 136T, 140; filial deprivation and, 48, 50, 52, 136T; helpful factors and, 136T; type of placement and, 138; visiting patterns and, 68, 136T; see also Reason for placement

Socioeconomic index, construction of, 15–17, 17n

Socioeconomic level of study families, 16–17; attitudes toward agencies and, 70, 80, 88; caseworker and, 65, 72, 107–8, 134; changes in family circumstances and, 20–23, 30–31; community

resources and, 86, 93, 134; evaluation of placement and, 59, 60T, 62, 72, 80, 134; family definition and, 124, 126; father contacts and, 127; filial deprivation and, 48, 52–53; household composition and, 121; placement status and, 30–31; policy implications and, 141; preventive services and, 91; role expectations and, 107–8, 114; visiting patterns and, 67

Srole anomie scale, 71, 71n

Stack, Carol B., 119–20, 120n

Study sample, characteristics of, 3–4, 6–12, 6T, 9T, 11T, 30, 57n, 96

Support, main source of: changes in family circumstances and, 20–23, 28, 30–31; placement status and, 30–31; variable in socioeconomic index, 15–16; see also Public assistance

Thomas, Edwin J., 96n, 97, 97n, 103, 103n

Timms, Noel, 107–8, 108n

Unwillingness or inability to assume care of child, 14, 35–36; see also Reason for placement, Socially acceptable or disapproved reasons for placement

Unwillingness or inability to continue care of child, 14, 38–39; see also Reason for placement, Socially acceptable or disapproved reasons for placement

Visits to child during placement, 65–69, 109; changes in family circumstances and, 30–31; demographic factors and, 67; maternal commitment and, 109; placement status and, 30–31; problems encountered, 67–69; reason for placement and, 67–68, 136T

Weiss, Carol, 90, 90n

Wilder vs. Sugarman, 104n

Wispé, L. G. A., 97, 97n

Worries about child during placement, 55–56, 110; maternal commitment and, 110

Related Titles in Child Welfare from Columbia

FILIAL DEPRIVATION AND FOSTER CARE
Shirley Jenkins and Elaine Norman

This is the first report on the most elaborate investigation of foster care ever undertaken. It describes family living, problems leading to placement, feelings and attitudes of mothers and fathers, and changes in their circumstances during placement. The concept of *filial deprivation* is introduced, i.e., the separation experiences of mothers and fathers when children enter foster care. There is a discussion of the policy and practice implications of the findings.

"An exhaustive study in an area of social work practice to which little attention has been given—namely, the parents who place their children in foster care."—*Social Casework*

"A significant contribution of special interest to social welfare workers at all levels and others associated with problems of foster care."—*Choice*

FOSTER CARE OF CHILDREN
Nurture and Treatment
Draza Kline and Helen-Mary Forbush Overstreet

This volume presents the basic principles, processes, and procedures of the placement of children in the context of the dynamic interplay among the participants and their environments. It provides the necessary foundation for all practitioners concerned with temporary and partial forms of physical separation of children and parents.

"This book is a valuable addition to the literature in the field of child placement. It makes a contribution to education as well as to practice."—*Social Service Review*

"*Foster Care of Children* is recommended for use by students and beginning workers who need to know the basic principles in child placing and also by more experienced practitioners."—*Social Casework*

COLUMBIA UNIVERSITY PRESS
New York and London

ISBN 0-231-03812-7   Printed in U.S.A.

Publications
of the Child Welfare and Family Welfare Research Program

Borgatta, Edgar F., and David Fanshel. "The Child Behavior Characteristics (CBC) Form: Revised Age-Specific Forms." *Multivariate Behavioral Research,* 5, (January 1970), 49–81.

Fanshel, David. "The Exit of Children from Foster Care: An Interim Research Report." *Child Welfare,* 50 (February 1971), 65–81.

———— "Parental Failure and Consequences for Children: The Drug Abusing Mother Whose Children Are in Foster Care." *American Journal of Public Health* (June 1974), 604–12.

———— "Parental Visiting of Children in Foster Care: Key to Discharge?" *Social Service Review,* 4 (forthcoming, December 1975).

———— "Status Changes of Children in Foster Care: Final Results of the Columbia University Longitudinal Study." *Child Welfare,* 55 (forthcoming, March 1976).

Fanshel, David, and Eugene B. Shinn. *Children in Foster Care: A Longitudinal Investigation.* New York: Columbia University Press (forthcoming).

———— *Dollars and Sense in the Foster Care of Children.* New York: Child Welfare League of America, 1972 (47 pages).

Jenkins, Shirley. "Filial Deprivation in Parents of Children in Foster Care." *Children,* 14 (January–February 1967), 8–12.

———— "Separation Experiences of Parents Whose Children Are in Foster Care." *Child Welfare,* 48 (June 1969), 334–40.

Jenkins, Shirley, and Elaine Norman. *Beyond Placement: Mothers View Foster Care.* New York: Columbia University Press, 1975 (152 pages).

———— "Families of Children in Foster Care." *Children,* 16 (July–August 1969), 155–59.

———— *Filial Deprivation and Foster Care.* New York: Columbia University Press, 1972 (296 pages).

Norman, Elaine. "Some Correlates of Behavioral Expectations: A Role Study of Mothers with Children in Foster Care Placement." Unpublished Ph.D. dissertation, City University of New York, 1972 (204 pages).

Shapiro, Deborah. *Agencies and Children: A Child Welfare Network's Investment in its Clients.* New York: Columbia University Press (in press).

———— "Agency Investment in Foster Care: A Follow-Up." *Social Work,* 18 (November 1973), 3–9.

———— "Agency Investment in Foster Care: A Study." *Social Work,* 17 (July 1972), 20–28.

———— "Occupational Mobility and Child Welfare Workers: An Exploratory Study." *Child Welfare,* 53 (January 1974), 5–13.

———— "Professional Education and the Child Welfare Worker: An Exploratory Study," in *Approaches to Innovation in Social Work Education.* New York: Council on Social Work Education, 1974; pp. 82–91.